SIMPLY MING
IN YOUR KITCHEN

SIMPLY MING
IN YOUR KITCHEN

80 Recipes to Watch, Learn, Cook & Enjoy

Ming Tsai and Arthur Boehm

Photography by Bill Bettencourt

KYLE BOOKS

Dedications

Ming Tsai
For my sons David and Henry, the two reasons I keep trying to make the world a happier place.

Arthur Boehm
For Richard Getke. And for C. and P.

Published in 2012 by Kyle Books
an imprint of Kyle Cathie Limited
www.kylebooks.com

Distributed by National Book Network
4501 Forbes Blvd., Suite 200
Lanham, MD 20706
Phone: (800) 462-6420
Fax: (301) 429-5746
custserv@nbnbooks.com

Project editor Anja Schmidt
Designer Jacqui Caulton
Photographer Bill Bettencourt
Prop styling Aaron Michael Caramanis
Copy editor Liana Krissoff
Production by Gemma John and Nic Jones

978-1-906868-73-4

Library of Congress Control No: 2012944604

Color Reproduction by Alta Image
Printed and bound in China by C & C Offset Ltd

Contents

Introduction

As a chef, I love bringing something new to the table. So I'm really happy to present this book. Not only does it deliver great, easy recipes, but for the first time you also get . . . me.

I'd better explain. Each of the recipes has its own accompanying video of me showing you how to make the dish. Which means you can have your own personal sous-chef, me again. You also get a complete shopping list for the recipe, so no more scribbled-on scraps of paper to bring to the store.

How did the book come about? All my adult life I've been teaching people how to cook, in my cookbooks and on my TV shows. I'm always thrilled when people approach me and tell me they love my dishes. (I'm happiest when people tell me they've tweaked my recipes, which means they're *really* cooking.) The books are about teaching and so are the shows. The shows add "pictures" to words. Now you get book and show in one. My tips on ingredients and techniques, the way I plate a dish, everything that's best conveyed through seeing, you can now see alongside this book.

But even without the videos, the book alone is a mighty tool. It's organized by food types, like seafood and poultry, and, as ever, it emphasizes simplicity and technique. For the first time, though, I've put my love of entertaining on the page in the form of three special chapters. The first, Platters, provides recipes for hors d'oeuvres and other starters that help make a party go. There's even a section that tells you how to conduct your own sushi-making party, for which your guests make and plate their own maki. I've had such parties and, believe me, they break the ice fast.

The other "entertaining" chapters are on sweets and cocktails. In Sweets, I present great party desserts like Lemongrass Panna Cotta and Cardamom Chocolate Cake. In Cocktails, I introduce some of the great drinks we make and serve at my restaurant Blue Ginger. If you want to start a party with a bang, any of my cocktails will do it. Mixed drinks are all the rage, and those I present, like the Sake Cucumber Martini and Passion Fruit Mai Tai, are rage-worthy indeed.

Many of us are eating less meat, or have given it up entirely. I've never thought of vegetable dishes as a compromise. Worldwide, the range of non-meat dishes is vast and delicious, and it's a great treat (as well as a challenge) to create my own contenders. Vegheads and meat-eaters alike will enjoy dishes like Hunan Glazed Eggplant with Rice and Three-Mushroom and Jicama Chow Mein.

Ultimately, my goal is to get people to cook. This book's innovations should encourage people to do just that. Nothing, I believe, is more rewarding than cooking for family and friends. The better people eat, the happier they are, and the happier they are, the better. I'm betting that this book will aid the cause.

How to use this book

It's easy and we've given you three ways:

1. Download a QR code reader to your mobile device, scan the QR code of the recipe you're interested in and you'll be taken to the In Your Kitchen landing page on ming.com, where you can sign up. Then you can download the recipe's shopping list for free and choose to watch the video. (The first two videos of each chapter are free; after that you pay only 99 cents per video.) You only need to sign up once—thereafter you'll be automatically directed to the recipe you desire.

2. No mobile device? No problem. Just type the URLs that run along the bottom of each recipe into your computer's browser and you'll get to the same place and sign up as above.

3. Most simply, go to ming.com and click on the In Your Kitchen tab and navigate from there.

Pantry

OILS AND VINEGARS

Canola Oil. My oil of choice for most cooking. Expressed from rapeseed, canola oil is lower in fat (it contains about 6 percent) than any other vegetable oil. It also contains omega-3 fatty acids. I prefer it not only for health reasons, but for its clean "neutral" flavor.

Rice Vinegar. A delicate, lightly acidic vinegar, white to golden in color. Rice vinegar should be naturally brewed and unflavored—check labels. I prefer organic brands, like Wan Ja Shan.

Truffle Oil. Made from olive oil or a mixture of olive and other oils, this versatile ingredient is infused with black or white truffles. It imparts a rich, earthy truffle flavor to a variety of savory dishes. The brand I like is Terre di Tartufo White Truffle Oil.

Toasted Sesame Oil. This amber-colored, richly flavored oil, a staple of the Chinese pantry, is used for seasoning only. Don't confuse it with refined, almost colorless sesame oils, which can be used for dressings and cooking.

NOODLES, RICE, AND WRAPPERS

Banana Leaves. These natural wrappers, used to enclose food for steaming, impart a subtle anise flavor. They come fresh or frozen—fresh are best. Rinse and dry fresh leaves before using them, and cut away fibrous stems. Defrost frozen leaves at room temperature and unfold them carefully. Wipe all banana leaves before using them with a damp cloth. Look for banana leaves among the frozen foods in Asian, Hispanic, or specialty markets.

Chow Mein Noodles. Fresh wheat-flour and egg noodles that are used to make chow mein and other dishes. Don't confuse these with the crisp noodles often served in Chinese-American restaurants for munching or to be sprinkled on stir-frys.

Lumpia Wrappers. Used traditionally in Philippine cooking to make spring rolls, these skins are made principally from flour, cornstarch and eggs. Sometimes sold as egg roll wrappers or spring roll shells, they're most often available in 11-ounce packages.

Mu Shu Wrappers. These round wrappers are made from wheat flour and tapioca starch. Usually sold frozen, defrost them at room temperature before using.

Mung Bean Noodles. Also called cellophane and bean thread noodles, these fine, translucent noodles are made from ground mung beans. The noodles are never cooked, but are soaked in water until pliable. They're sold dry in packages that range from 1 ounce to 1 pound.

Nori. These thin dried seaweed sheets are used primarily to make maki, the Japanese rolls that contain rice and other fillings. Buy toasted nori (labeled *yaki nori*), which are sold flat in packages. Iridescent black, dark green, or purplish, nori, if not used immediately, should be wrapped in plastic and stored in a cool, dark place.

Rice Stick Noodles. This widely available thin, flat noodle is one of a large family of rice noodles, both fresh and dried.

Rice Vermicelli. Long, thin and round, these noodles take their English name from the Italian pasta called "little worms." They're mostly available in 1-pound bags.

Shanghai Noodles. An egg noodle that's medium thin and usually sold in 1-pound bags. If you can't find them, substitute any thick dried or fresh spaghetti.

Rice Paper Wrappers. Known also as *banh trang*, these Vietnamese wrappers are made from a rice plant product. They're used for preparing spring rolls, uncooked or fried. They're most commonly available in 12-ounce packages of 8 round wrappers, and must be soaked briefly before using.

Sushi Rice. Ideal for making sushi because of its moderately sticky texture when cooked, short-grained sushi rice is widely available. Calrose and Kokuho are two brands of American-grown sushi rice. Labeling is sometimes inexact. "Japanese rice," "new rice," or "variety rice" are "sushi rice" alternatives. The most highly regarded Japanese sushi rice is *koshihikari* and is produced domestically.

Wonton Wrappers. Flour- and egg-based, these skins come round or square, thick or thin. Wontons require round skins. I recommend the thinnest ones you can find, usually labeled "extra thin." The skins can be refrigerated for up to 1 week, or frozen for about 2 months. I prefer Twin Marquis brand.

SEASONINGS, CONDIMENTS AND AROMATICS

Agave Syrup. Produced in Mexico and South Africa, this product of the agave plant, which is also used to make Tequila, is similar to honey, but lighter and more "neutral" in taste. There are two kinds of the syrup, sometimes sold as agave "nectar," light and dark. The former is milder, and the one I recommend for the recipes in this book.

Fermented Black Beans. This pungent ingredient, used throughout China, is made from partially decomposed soybeans that are dried and then salted. Sold most often in plastic bags, they last indefinitely if stored in a cool, lightless place. Rinse the beans before using to remove excess salt.

Five-Spice Powder. A traditional Chinese seasoning blend usually composed of equal parts ground cinnamon, star anise, cloves, fennel and Szechuan peppercorns. With a fragrant, "warm-cool" flavor, the spice goes particularly well with fatty meats like pork and duck. The spice is thought to be healthful, as the number five is considered meaningful in Chinese belief.

Fish Sauce. Called *nam pla* in Thailand and *noc mam* in Vietnam, this Southeast Asian staple is made from salted and fermented anchovies. I prefer the Thai Three Crabs brand, which has a clean sea taste and is less sweet than others I've tried. Once opened, keep fish sauce in the fridge.

Chinese Hot Mustard Powder. The ground product of pungent mustard seeds, this is mixed with water before using. It's available in some supermarkets and Asian food stores.

Ketjap Manis. A syrupy, dark brown Indonesian seasoning made from soybeans, palm sugar, and other ingredients, including garlic. Similar to soy sauce, but sweeter and with a more complex flavor than most soy-sauce types, it's available in Asian markets.

Korean Chile Pepper Flakes. Known in Korea as *gochugaru*, this incendiary seasoning is made from sun-dried thin chiles. It's available in Asian markets. Once opened, store the pepper in a jar in the fridge.

Madras Curry Powder. All curry powders are spice blends. My preferred type and brand is labeled "Madras curry powder," a mixture that's favored in the southern Indian state from which it derives its name. It has a mellow balance that's neither too hot nor too mild. Look for brands in which bits of bay leaf are visible, and use it only when it's fresh.

Mirin. This essential Japanese ingredient is made from rice wine and sugar. It adds a touch of sweetness to many dishes and is also used as a glaze. I recommend naturally brewed *hon-mirin*. It contains natural sugars rather than sweeteners like corn syrup, which is found in *agi-mirin*, an alternative type.

Miso. The defining ingredient of the eponymous Japanese soup, miso is a savory seasoning paste made from rice, barley, and/or soybeans. For the recipes in this book, I call for *shiro miso*, which is made from rice. It's available in cans, jars, tubs and plastic bags, and is best stored in the fridge, where it lasts up to 3 months.

Natural Garlic Powder. The FDA maintains that the word "natural" on products including garlic and onion powders may be used if the product contains no artificial flavors or other synthetic substances. In my experience, natural garlic powder, which is free from additives, is superior to other kinds, which can be acrid or otherwise taste "off." I use natural garlic and onion powders for spice rubs, where the fresh kind would not work as well, if at all. All garlic and onion powders must be fresh.

Organic Worcestershire Sauce. Most of us are familiar with traditional Worcestershire sauce, a piquant tamarind-based flavoring and condiment. Recipes for the commercial organic type vary widely, but the sauce usually contains the defining tamarind, soy or tamari sauce, vinegar and sweeteners. The brand I prefer is Wan Ja Shan.

Pickled Ginger. Most notably used as a sushi condiment, pickled ginger, or *gari,* is thinly sliced ginger preserved in sweet vinegar or a vinegar-sugar solution. It's widely available in Asian markets and at some supermarkets.

Sambal. A fiery, chile-based condiment from Southeast Asia, the type I use, and which you're most likely to find, is *sambal oelek.* It's usually made from chiles, vinegar, sugar and salt and is without other ingredients, such as garlic and shrimp paste, found in other sambal types.

Shoyu Ponzu. This thin citrus-based Japanese sauce with added soy or tamari sauce is also made with ingredients that can include mirin, rice vinegar, *katsobushi* (dried fermented tuna) and seaweed. I use a naturally brewed, wheat-free, tamari-based sauce made by Wan Ja Shan.

Soy Sauce. The indispensable Chinese and Japanese seasoning, soy sauce has been used for millennia. I call for naturally brewed "regular" soy sauce, which is sometimes called light or thin to distinguish it from darker or thicker kinds. Soy sauce is made from a soybean, flour

and water mixture and should be naturally fermented or brewed rather than synthetically or chemically produced. Look for "naturally brewed" on the label and read ingredient listings. Avoid soy sauces that contain hydrolyzed soy protein, corn syrup and caramel color—a sure sign of an ersatz sauce. Japanese Kikkoman soy sauce is a standby, but I prefer an organic brand like Wan Ja Shan.

Sriracha. A Thai hot sauce made with chiles, garlic salt and vinegar, sriracha has the consistency of ketchup, and varies in heat, from super-hot to mild. American-made Huy Fong, which comes in a squeeze bottle, is definitely on the hotter side of the spectrum, and a brand I commonly use.

Tamari . Sometimes confused with soy sauce, tamari is also soybean-based, but darker and richer than regular soy sauce. I call for wheat-free tamari, sometimes labeled "organic, wheat-free," which I prefer for its pure good taste. Check labels to assure yourself of wheat-free tamari. Wan Ja Shan is my brand of choice.

Thai Basil. Native to Southeast Asia, the plant has narrow leaves and purplish stems and a sweet licorice taste with lemon undertones. I love its exotic flavor, which I find more interesting than the regular kind; I also find that it retains its fragrance in cooking to a greater degree than sweet basil.

Togarashi. Japanese chiles that are available fresh or dried, and also dried and ground. The latter is required for the recipes in this book, and can be found in bottles in Asian markets.

Vegetarian Oyster Sauce. Regular oyster sauce is a versatile Chinese ingredient made from cooked fresh oysters that are seasoned with soy sauce, salt and spices. Though its slightly fishy taste dissipates in cooking, some people would rather forgo oysters entirely. For them I recommend vegetarian oyster sauce, which is made from shiitake mushrooms rather than oysters—a sensible substitution, as both are umami-rich. I prefer the Wan Ja Shan brand.

Vegetarian Stir-Fry Sauce. Used as a flavoring finish for stir-frys, this sauce sometimes contains its own thickening agent and most contain soy sauce. I prefer the mushroom-based kind made by Wan Ja Shen.

OTHER INGREDIENTS

Chinese Sausages. Called *lap chong*, these small, thin dried sausages are made from pork or duck; the former is the kind you're most likely to find. *Lap chong* are sweetened and often steamed before using. Buy them in Chinese markets or in some meat stores.

Couscous. This staple of North African cuisine, a kind of pasta, is made from coarsely ground semolina mixed with water and then dried. Two types are available—the pre-steamed "instant" kind and the traditional variety that must be steamed to cook to fluffiness. The traditional kind is used for recipes in this book. Couscous also comes in three grain sizes: coarse, medium and fine—medium is most typical—and in whole-wheat versions. Buy couscous packaged or from Middle Eastern and natural food stores in bulk.

Ground Dark Turkey or Chicken Meat. Available at butcher shops, supermarkets and online, this versatile, relatively low-fat product makes flavorful burgers and meatloaf.

Panko. Because these Japanese breadcrumbs are large and flat, they coat foods for frying and sautéing better, resulting in delicately crunchy crusts. Panko is widely available in Asian stores and many supermarkets.

Rice Flour. This gluten-free powdery flour is typically used for baking, but also makes a superior batter for coating seafood and vegetables for frying. Rice flour is widely available.

Seitan and Tempeh. Two versatile, protein-rich foods with firm chewy textures that are good substitutes for meat in stir-frys and other dishes, where they readily pick up flavors. Seitan is made from wheat gluten and is available in packages or tubs in the refrigerator section of natural food stores and Asian markets. Tempeh, a soybean product, is also available in packages, fresh or frozen, at the same stores and at some supermarkets.

Tea-Smoked Salmon. We make our own tea-smoked salmon at Blue Ginger, and so can you, but this wonderfully flavored ingredient can also be bought.

Tofu. An ancient Chinese and Japanese product that's prepared from curdled soymilk in a process similar to cheesemaking. It comes in extra-firm, firm, soft and silken styles, and is also available smoked. Silken tofu is the most delicate. Rich in protein and low in fat and cholesterol-free, tofu is extremely nutritious. Though sold fresh in water, it's most commonly available in packages or tubs. Refrigerate unused portions in the original container, or transfer to water and refresh daily.

TECHNIQUES AND OTHER MATTERS

Brining. I like to brine pork before cooking it (ditto chicken and turkey for Thanksgiving) and recommend you do too. The process, which involves soaking meat or poultry in a solution of salt, water and sugar, enhances taste and maximizes juiciness. It works because the brined item absorbs and retains the soaking liquid. Brining instructions appear in the respective recipes.

Food Sensitivities. To avoid potential allergic reactions, work smart. Always clean your cutting board and knife between jobs. If, for example, I'm chopping nuts, I reflexively wash my board and knife before chopping another ingredient. Keeping your board and knife clean this way also avoids cross-contamination—the transfer of bacteria from raw ingredients to cooked ones. This is particularly important when you're having guests whose food sensitivities you—or they—may not know.

Heating the Pan. To minimize the possibility of sticking, all my recipes direct that a pan used for browning be heated before adding oil. Following this method, the oil is in contact with the pan for less time and is thus less likely to break down—to become viscous and gummy and thus sticky. Even a trace of broken-down oil can contribute to sticking.

Making Rice. To make perfectly cooked rice every time, I recommend using a rice cooker, as millions of

Asians do, and the rice can be held hot in the cooker for up to 8 hours. For making white or brown rice, or a combination, I always use the "Mt. Fuji" method, which involves using your hand to determine how much water is needed in relation to the rice (see 50-50 White and Brown Rice for 4 Servings, below).

Organic Poultry and Meat. I always advise cooks to seek out meat and poultry that's certified organic—or is labeled in such a way to indicate that the animal has been humanely raised, without hormones or growth promotants, and on wholesome feed. As for poultry, I specify that the birds be free-range. Because of the care given to birds destined for the kosher table, I also recommend kosher chicken and meat products. The label "naturally raised" indicates that the product has met USDA-established standards for animal wellbeing and health. If you can, buy meat and poultry that's been locally processed by small producers, which are usually more conscientious about animal welfare than mass-manufacturers. The payoff for such choosiness is more healthful, more flavorful eating.

Seasoning. My recipes call for frequent seasoning adjustments, as necessary—"correcting" salt and pepper, and other seasonings, as you cook. This means tasting a dish frequently while cooking—repeated tasting is basic to ensuring a delicious result. Please understand that I don't advise overloading a dish with one seasoning or another, but rather bringing it to its maximum flavor potential through judicious seasoning adjustment.

Sustainable Tuna. I always recommend that cooks buy sustainable tuna, which comes from a fishery with practices that don't reduce the species' ability to maintain its population, and that don't negatively affect the food source of other species or damage their environment. Tuna should be caught by troll or "pole and line"—using fishing pole and bait—rather than by long lines, which use baited hooks attached at intervals. There are other criteria for sustainable fishing. Always ask the person from whom you buy tuna where and how the fish was caught. If they don't know or you don't get a satisfying answer, shop elsewhere. For futher information go to seafoodwatch.com.

50-50 WHITE AND BROWN RICE FOR 4 SERVINGS (8 CUPS)

Rinse 1½ cups brown rice and soak it in fresh cold water to cover for 1 hour. Transfer the rice to a medium saucepan.

Put 1½ cups white rice in a large bowl in the sink. Rinse the rice by filling the bowl with cold water and stirring the rice with your hand. Drain and repeat until the water in the bowl is clean. Transfer the rice to the same saucepan.

Flatten the rice with your palm and without removing it, add water until it touches the highest knuckle of your middle finger. Cover and boil over high heat for 10 minutes. Lower the heat to medium and simmer for 30 minutes. Turn off the heat and let the rice stand, covered, to plump, for 20 minutes. Stir gently and serve.

Ming's Tip

To store cooked rice to be used for fried rice, spread it out in a thin layer on a clean baking sheet. Refrigerate, uncovered, overnight and break up any clumps before adding to a stir-fried rice recipe. If short on time, place the baking sheet in the freezer for 30 minutes, checking the rice periodically to make sure it doesn't freeze.

CHAPTER 1

Platters

Platters should invite sociability, and the ones here do just that. Placed on a coffee or buffet table, bar or kitchen counter, they bring people together. And many can be prepared ahead, frozen and finished before serving. That's social security in the freezer.

Party bites must be delicious. Crispy Vegetable Spring Rolls, which feature caramelized onions and crunchy carrots, and Shrimp and Mango Summer Rolls—hot, sweet and cooling—make an instant impression. So do luscious Honey Crab Wontons and Pan-Fried Scallop Satays with Bacon and Black Bean Aioli, an update of the beloved bacon and scallop duo.

I like to surprise guests with novel presentations. Onion-Burger "Hot Dogs" with Sweet Chile Relish—hot dog–shaped burgers served in hot dog rolls—always delight. So does Work-Stirred Tuna Poke on Sushi Rice, which are presented in Chinese spoons, and Parsnip Purée with Curry-Ginger Oil, offered in espresso cups. Smashed Shrimp Shumai—shrimp-mousse dumplings, flattened for manageability—invite happy nibbling.

I'm particularly proud of my Sushi Rolling Party, which offers four maki recipes that guests make and plate themselves. The rolling is lots of fun and, no matter how unchefly the result, everyone digs in. Another way that platters make good times happen.

Spring rolls are the perfect party food. Delicious and easily handled—you can cut them into bite-size pieces—they invite happy munching. These fried vegetable rolls, which feature caramelized onions and shredded carrot, also make a perfect counterpoint to meat- or seafood-based hors d'oeuvres.

I use lumpia to wrap these—Philippine skins that, I've found, make the crispest, most delicate spring rolls. You can find them at many Asian markets. A final lettuce wrap adds more textural excitement.

CRISPY VEGETABLE SPRING ROLLS

MAKES 15

1 package (about 9 ounces) rice vermicelli or bean thread noodles

1 tablespoon canola oil, plus more for frying

2 large onions, sliced ¼ inch thick

Kosher salt and freshly ground black pepper

1 tablespoon minced ginger

1 tablespoon minced garlic

1 head Bibb lettuce, separated into leaves

½ cup hoisin sauce

2 cups shredded carrots

10 to 12 square lumpia wrappers

1 egg beaten with 1 tablespoon water, for egg wash

Leaves from 1 bunch mint

DIM SUM DIPPER

1 tablespoon sambal

3 tablespoons rice vinegar

2 tablespoons naturally brewed soy sauce

To Drink:

A Champagne or sparkling wine like Veuve Clicquot, Schramsberg Brut Rose or 90+ Prosecco

1 Put the noodles in a large bowl and fill it with hot water to cover. When the noodles have softened, after about 15 minutes for rice vermicelli, or 10 minutes for bean threads, drain and chop roughly. Measure 3 cups noodles and set aside.

2 Heat a large sauté pan over medium heat. Add the 1 tablespoon oil and swirl to coat the pan. When the oil is hot, add the onions. Season with salt and pepper, flip to incorporate, then add the ginger and garlic. Don't stir so the onions can caramelize, about 5 minutes.

3 Meanwhile, make the dipper: In a small bowl, combine the sambal, vinegar and soy sauce, and set aside. Prepare the lettuce wrappers by picking out 10 to 12 large leaves from the inner third of the lettuce.

4 Flip the onions and cook for another 5 minutes on the other side. Add the hoisin sauce to the caramelized onions and cook, stirring, for 1 minute. Transfer the mixture to a medium bowl, add the noodles and carrots, season with salt and pepper, and stir to combine. Cool.

5 To make the rolls, place a wrapper on a work surface with a corner near you. Place 2 heaping tablespoons of the filling a little above the corner and bring the near corner of the wrapper over the filling to enclose it. Brush the edges with the egg wash, roll to the middle of the wrapper, fold in the sides, and continue to roll. Rest the roll seam side down and repeat with the remaining wrappers and filling.

6 Fill a fryer or medium heavy pot one-third full with oil. Over high heat, bring to 375°F on a deep-frying thermometer. Gently drop half the rolls into the oil and fry until golden brown, about 5 minutes. Remove with a large mesh spoon and drain on paper towels. Repeat with the remaining rolls.

7 To serve, place a roll at the bottom of a lettuce leaf. Place 2 mint leaves on top and roll to enclose as you did previously. Transfer the rolls to a platter and serve with the dipper.

Ming's tip:

To make these in advance, fry the rolls until pale gold, 3 to 4 minutes, drain them, and let them cool to room temperature. Transfer the rolls to resealable plastic bags and freeze, up to 2 weeks. When ready to serve, fry them again still frozen   be on guard for splattering as you add them to the oil— until golden, about 2 minutes, and transfer them to a colander. Allow heat to penetrate their interiors, about 4 minutes. Return the rolls to the fryer to recrisp, about 1 minute, drain, wrap in the lettuce, and serve.

I call these light, fresh-tasting rolls summer rolls because they feature basil, an herb I associate with that season. Mangos, a warm-weather fruit, add tropical allure, and nicely accent the sweetness of the shrimp. Sambal adds heat, which is "cooled" by fresh mint. In other words, this dish is a party for your mouth. I like to wrap these in rice paper, but, for simplicity and even more freshness, you can use lettuce leaves instead.

SHRIMP AND MANGO SUMMER ROLLS

MAKES 8

Kosher salt

16 medium shrimp, peeled, deveined and halved lengthwise

2 medium ripe mangos, peeled, pitted, halved, and sliced ⅛ inch thick

Juice of 2 limes

1 tablespoon fish sauce

1 teaspoon sambal or hot sauce, or to taste

Freshly ground black pepper

8 rice paper wrappers or 8 Bibb lettuce leaves

Leaves from 1 bunch Thai basil or regular basil

1 Fill a large bowl with water and add ice cubes. Bring a large saucepan of salted water to a boil, add the shrimp and blanch until just cooked through, 30 seconds to 1 minute. Drain and transfer to the bowl with ice water to stop the cooking. Immediately drain the shrimp and transfer to a medium bowl. Add the mangos, lime juice, fish sauce, and sambal, season with pepper, and stir to combine.

2 Soften the rice paper wrappers, if using: Place 1 in a circular baking dish and cover with hot water. Soak until just softened, 15 to 30 seconds. Transfer the wrapper to a lint-free towel to drain, top with a second towel and blot dry. Transfer the rice paper to a flat surface, place 4 pieces of shrimp from the filling across the center of the wrapper, and top with one-eighth of the filling. Top with 3 or 4 basil leaves and roll, folding in the sides halfway through. Alternatively, roll using lettuce leaves. Repeat with the remaining rice paper or lettuce leaves, shrimp and filling.

3 Halve each roll on the diagonal and serve immediately.

Ming's tip:

These can prepared ahead of time and placed in a rectangular storage container. Cover the rolls with a damp towel, cover it with plastic wrap, then snap on the lid. Refrigerate and bring to room temperature before serving.

Video tip:

Watch the video for my trick to using rice paper wrappers.

To Drink:

A New World Sauvignon Blanc, like Wither Hills, from New Zealand

I've based these on crab rangoon, the deep-fried, crab-filled dumplings of Chinese-American restaurant cooking. Often made with imitation crab and too much cream cheese, they can fall below the mark. Not, however, my super version, made with the best crab, a touch of honey, jicama for crunch, and just enough cream cheese for richness. A perfect party nibble, these can be formed in advance, held in the fridge, and fried just before serving.

HONEY CRAB WONTONS

MAKES ABOUT 40

1 pound Maine crabmeat, or other lump crabmeat

2 tablespoons honey

1 cup peeled and diced jicama

3 tablespoons thinly sliced chives

cup cream cheese, at room temperature

Kosher salt and freshly ground black pepper

1 package thin square wonton wrappers

1 egg beaten with 1 tablespoon water, for egg wash

Canola oil for frying

1 In a medium bowl, combine the crabmeat, 1 tablespoon of the honey, the jicama, 2 tablespoons of the chives and the cream cheese. Season with salt and pepper and blend.

2 Place 1 wonton wrapper on a work surface with 1 corner nearest you. Place 1 scant tablespoon of the filling in the center of the wrapper, moisten the edges with the egg wash, and fold the bottom half over the top to create a triangular dumpling. Bring the left and right sides under the dumpling, moisten the points with the egg wash, and pinch together to seal. Repeat with the remaining wrappers and filling.

3 Fill a fryer or medium heavy pot one-third full with oil. Over high heat, bring to 350°F on a deep-frying thermometer. Add half the wontons and fry until golden brown, about 2 minutes. Remove with a large mesh spoon and drain on paper towels. Repeat with the remaining wontons.

4 Transfer to a platter, drizzle with the remaining 1 tablespoon honey, sprinkle with the remaining chives, and serve.

Ming's tip:

Don't overfill the wontons or they won't seal properly.

Video tips:

Watch the video to see my simple technique for peeling and dicing jicama and to learn how to form the wontons.

To Drink:

An off-dry Semillon or a Fiano de Avellino, like Feudi San Gregorio, from Italy

Grilled skewered food is irresistible. Satays—the snack-size Indonesian version—also make terrific party bites, as they're easily handled as well as delicious. These satays feature chicken breasts, marinated first for exciting flavor, and a basil purée garnish. I think of the purée as a quickly done pesto; it's a great flavoring "drizzle" to keep in mind for garnishing soups or as a pasta sauce. For serving ease, the purée also eliminates the need to pass a separate sauce.

GRILLED GARLIC CHICKEN SATAYS
with Basil Purée

MAKES 18

2 tablespoons minced garlic, plus 2 cloves for the purée

3 tablespoons canola oil, plus more for brushing the grill

2 tablespoons naturally brewed soy sauce

Freshly ground black pepper

3 boneless, skinless chicken breasts (about 1½ pounds), tenders removed, see Tip

Kosher salt

Leaves from 1 bunch basil

½ cup extra-virgin olive oil

Banana leaf or shredded cabbage or iceberg lettuce

Eighteen 6- to 8-inch wooden skewers

1 In a medium bowl, combine the 2 tablespoons garlic, 3 tablespoons canola oil and the soy sauce. Season the marinade with pepper and stir.

2 Butterfly each chicken breast by placing it with the thin end nearest to you. With a palm resting on the breast, run a knife parallel to your work surface through the thickest side of the breast and open like a book. Cut each breast into 6 equal vertical strips. Add the strips and tenders to the marinade, turn to coat, and refrigerate for 1 to 2 hours. Meanwhile, soak the skewers in a bowl of water for 1 hour.

3 Remove the chicken from the marinade and thread a skewer straight through each strip. Preheat an outdoor grill or broiler or use a large grill pan. If broiling, cover a baking sheet with foil and set the rack in the middle.

4 Fill a large bowl with water and add ice cubes. Bring a large pot of salted water to a boil. Add the basil and blanch until the leaves are bright green, 30 seconds to 1 minute. Drain the basil in a large sieve and transfer the strainer with the leaves to the bowl with ice water. When the basil is cold, drain and squeeze the leaves to remove all the water. Transfer to a blender. Add the 2 cloves garlic to the blender and blend, drizzling in the olive oil to make a purée. Add 2 tablespoons water, or more, so the mixture can be drizzled. Season with salt and pepper and set aside.

5 Brush the grill, grill pan, or baking sheet with canola oil. Season the chicken with salt and pepper and grill or broil, or cook in the grill pan, turningé once, until the chicken is cooked through, 2 to 3 minutes per side.

6 Place the banana leaf, or spread the cabbage or lettuce, on a serving platter. Top with the satays, drizzle with the purée and serve.

To Drink:

A Rioja, like Faustino VII

Ming's tip:

You can also use the breast tenders to make chicken fingers. I bread the tenders with panko, which makes the most delicate crust.

Video tip:

Watch the video to learn how to butterfly chicken breasts.

I'm a golfing fiend. For a while, I spent as much time as I could golfing at the Olympic Club in San Francisco. One of its attractions, besides the course itself, was its signature dish, hot dog–shaped burgers served in hot dog buns, garnished with a fantastic chile sauce. Here's my version, which makes another great party nibble. The burger shape is the same, but I've upped the ante by adding onions to the beef and making sure the sauce has an intense spicy-sweet tang. Serve this with your favorite chips.

ONION-BURGER "HOT DOGS"
with Sweet Chile Relish

MAKES 8

3 tablespoons canola oil
2 large onions, minced
Kosher salt and freshly ground
    black pepper
1 tablespoon minced garlic
1 large red bell pepper, minced
1 tablespoon sambal or hot sauce,
    or to taste
2 tablespoons agave syrup
    or honey
½ cup rice vinegar
1 tablespoon cornstarch mixed
    with 1 tablespoon cold water
2 pounds ground beef
4 tablespoons unsalted butter
8 hot dog buns

1 Heat a large heavy skillet over medium heat. Add 1 tablespoon of the oil and swirl to coat the pan. When the oil is hot, add the onions, season with salt and pepper, and brown, without stirring, 5 to 6 minutes. Turn and brown for another 3 to 4 minutes. Transfer half the onions to a large bowl and cool.

2 Meanwhile, add the garlic to the skillet, season with salt and pepper, and sauté, stirring, for 1 minute. Add the red pepper and sauté, stirring, for 30 seconds, then add the sambal and agave, stir, and add the vinegar. Bring to a simmer, whisk in the cornstarch slurry, and simmer until the relish is thickened, about 30 seconds. Transfer to a bowl and cool to room temperature. Wipe out the skillet.

3 Put the beef in a large bowl and add the reserved onions, season with salt and pepper, and combine lightly. Very gently shape the beef mixture into 8 thick ovals the length of the buns, and flatten the tops. Season with salt and pepper. Heat the skillet over medium-high heat, add the remaining 2 tablespoons oil, and swirl to coat the pan. When the oil is hot, add the beef patties and cook, turning once, about 4 minutes per side for medium-rare, 1 minute more per side for medium, and 1 minute more per side for medium-well.

4 Meanwhile, heat 2 tablespoons of the butter in a medium pan over medium-high heat. When the butter has melted, add half the hot dog buns crumb side down and toast, moving them in the butter, until brown and crisp, about 1 minute. Repeat with the remaining 2 tablespoons butter and buns.

5 Transfer the "hot dogs" to the buns and cover generously with the relish. Transfer to a platter and serve.

To Drink:

A Syrah blend, like Arrogant Frog Croak Rotie Syrah Viognier, from France

Ming's tips:

You can make the relish and store it overnight, refrigerated.

You can toast the rolls without butter in a toaster, toaster oven, or under the broiler, if you like.

Pork and rice-noodle salad, seasoned with lemongrass and served on lettuce, is a Vietnamese treat. My version, which features pork patties, has extra zing due to jalapeño heat, and makes a terrific party dish. The textural contrasts—slithery noodles, chewy meat, crisp lettuce—really make diners happy, including those from the younger generation.

LEMONGRASS PORK LETTUCE CUP

MAKES 8

1 small package (about 7 ounces) rice vermicelli

Juice of 1 lime

2 tablespoons fish sauce

1 bunch scallions, white and green parts separated, thinly sliced

2 tablespoons canola oil

1 tablespoon minced ginger

2 tablespoons minced lemongrass, white part only (see Tip, page 166)

1 jalapeño pepper, minced

Kosher salt and freshly ground black pepper

1 pound ground pork

1 large head iceberg lettuce

1 Put the noodles in a medium bowl and fill it with hot water to cover. When the noodles have softened, after about 15 minutes, drain and measure 3 packed cups of noodles. Return the noodles to the bowl and add the lime juice, fish sauce and scallion greens, toss, and set aside.

2 Heat a medium heavy skillet over medium heat. Add 1 tablespoon of the oil and swirl to coat the pan. When the oil is hot, add the scallion whites, ginger, lemongrass, and jalapeño. Sauté, stirring, until the vegetables are soft, about 2 minutes. Transfer to a medium bowl and cool. Wipe out the skillet.

3 Add the pork to the bowl, season with salt and pepper and mix lightly. With wet hands, form 8 oval patties about ½ inch thick. Heat the skillet over medium-high heat, add the remaining 1 tablespoon oil, and swirl to coat the pan. When the oil is hot, add the patties and cook until browned, turning once, 3 to 4 minutes per side.

4 Pick 8 nice lettuce cups from a third of the way into your iceberg head. Place 1 piece of lettuce on your work surface. Top with one-eighth of the noodle salad and a patty. Repeat with the remaining lettuce, salad and patties. Transfer to a platter, garnish with the scallion greens and serve.

Video tip:

Watch the video to see my demonstration of mincing lemongrass.

To Drink:

An unoaked Chardonnay, like Caymus Mer Soleil Silver Santa Lucia Highlands

Anyone who pooh-poohs eggplant—and I've met too many who do—hasn't tasted eggplant caviar my way. Smoky and seriously garlic-flavored, it's served with chips made from pita bread that's first sprinkled with curry powder—a terrific combination, to say the least. I usually serve the caviar as a dip, surrounded by the chips, but you can also plate the chips and dollop the caviar on them. The recipe makes a good quantity of caviar, but having extra in the fridge for later enjoyment isn't a problem, believe me.

ROASTED EGGPLANT CAVIAR
with Curry Pita Chips

MAKES 24 CHIPS AND 4 CUPS CAVIAR

2 large eggplants
3 small or 2 large heads garlic
3 tablespoons extra-virgin olive oil, plus more for drizzling and brushing
Kosher salt and freshly ground black pepper
4 whole-wheat pita breads
1 tablespoon curry powder
1 bunch scallions, white and green parts separated, thinly sliced
½ cup balsamic vinegar

1 Preheat the oven to 400°F. Put the eggplants on a large baking tray. Cut the tops off the garlic heads, drizzle with oil, season with salt and pepper, and wrap each in foil. Transfer to the baking tray and roast the eggplants and garlic until soft, about 1 hour. Cool.

2 Lower the oven temperature to 350°F. Brush both sides of each pita bread lightly with oil, sprinkle with the curry powder, and season with salt. Halve each bread vertically then cut each half into thirds. Place the chips on a baking sheet and bake until crisp, turning once, 15 to 20 minutes.

3 When the eggplant can be handled, halve the eggplants and scoop the flesh into a food processor. Squeeze the garlic from the cloves into the processor, add the scallion whites, season with salt and pepper, and purée, drizzling in the 3 tablespoons oil. Adjust the seasoning and transfer the caviar to a serving bowl.

4 In a small nonreactive saucepan, bring the vinegar to a boil. Lower the heat and simmer until the vinegar is reduced to a syrupy consistency, 2 to 3 minutes.

5 Place the caviar in a bowl. Sprinkle with the scallion greens and surround with the chips. Drizzle the syrup over the caviar and chips and serve.

Ming's tip:

The caviar also makes a great filling for ravioli made with wonton wrappers. You can boil or pan-sear them.

To Drink:

A French Pinot Noir, like Louis Latour Domaine de Valmossine

SUSHI ROLLING PARTY

A sushi rolling party is fun for everyone. Guests really get into the easily mastered process of making maki, then enjoy the result of everyone's efforts, no matter how non-pro.

The host should prepare the sushi rice beforehand and keep it warm in a temperature-holding container like the Igloo sushi restaurants favor or in a glass or metal bowl covered with plastic wrap then foil. Bring the rice to your rolling area, a large table or kitchen island, for example.

Do your *mise en place*—prep all the recipes you'll use up to the point of rolling, including the water-vinegar mixture used for making the maki and handrolls. Place all ingredients in suitable dishes or small bowls that can be brought to the rolling area.

I like to have a rolling mat for each person—they're inexpensive—but you can certainly get away with fewer, depending on the number of guests. You'll also want to have slicing knives on hand to cut the rolls—straight across into eight pieces, on the bias into thirds, or any way you like—and a platter or platters lined with banana leaves or shredded cabbage or shredded iceberg lettuce for serving the sushi. Dishes of soy sauce, wasabi, and pickled ginger, the traditional sushi condiments, should also be on hand.

When everyone has gathered, demonstrate the rolling process—and your guests are in business.

To Drink:
A Riesling blend, like Cameron Hughes Lot 259 for all but the fennel chicken maki. For it, a Pinot Noir, like Cloudline, from Oregon, and/or Botani Moscatel from Spain

You'll need two batches of this recipe if you're planning a full party with all four maki recipes. One batch will get you through two maki recipes; halve this and you can make a party of one maki recipe.

SUSHI RICE

16 CUPS

1 Place 8 cups of short-grain sushi rice in a bowl or large-capacity rice-cooker insert and add water to cover it generously. Swish the rice in a single direction to rinse off residual starch. Drain, refill the bowl or insert, and swish again. Rinse and repeat 3 or 4 times until the water is clear.

2 Drain the rice and, if not using a rice cooker, transfer it to a large pot with a tight lid. If using a rice cooker, dry the outside of the insert and place it in the cooker. Flatten the rice with a palm and without removing your hand, add water until it just touches the highest knuckle of your middle finger. In the pot, fill with water the same way, cover and bring the water to a boil over high heat, about 15 minutes. Reduce the heat to medium-high and simmer for 20 to 25 minutes. Turn off the heat and let the rice stand, covered, to plump, 10 to 15 minutes. If using a rice cooker, turn it on.

3 Meanwhile, in a small nonreactive saucepan, combine 2 cups rice vinegar, ½ cup mirin and 1 cup sugar and heat until hot, about 5 minutes; don't allow the mixture to boil. Keep hot.

4 Invert the rice into a large stainless-steel or wooden bowl. (Don't include any browned bits that may have formed at the bottom of the pot.) Using a wooden or rubber spatula, gently fold half the vinegar mixture into the rice using a light, lifting motion to avoid mashing the rice. Taste; the rice should have a pleasingly sweet-acidic edge. If not, fold in more of the vinegar mixture.

5 Dampen a clean dish towel. With your hands, gently push the rice together to form a loose mound. Cover with the towel and let the rice rest for 20 minutes to develop its flavor. Store any leftovers in the refrigerator for up to 3 days.

Tuna is among the most popular sushi ingredients. Here, top-grade tuna is tossed in a chile-honey mixture, then made into deliciously hot-sweet rolls.

SPICY TUNA MAKI

MAKES 8 ROLLS

1 serrano chile, minced, or to taste

1 tablespoon honey

1 teaspoon naturally brewed soy sauce, plus additional for serving

1 tablespoon thinly sliced chives

8 ounces sashimi-grade tuna, preferably big eye, diced

Kosher salt and freshly ground black pepper

1 tablespoon rice vinegar mixed with 1 cup water, for rolling

8 cups Sushi Rice (opposite)

8 toasted nori sheets, halved lengthwise

Naturally brewed soy sauce

Wasabi

Sliced pickled ginger

1 In a medium bowl, combine the chile, honey, soy sauce, chives and tuna. Season with salt and pepper and gently mix.

2 To roll the sushi, have the vinegar-water mixture and sushi rice handy. Place a half sheet of the nori vertically on a work surface, shiny side down. With wet hands, pat 1 cup rice evenly over the bottom half of the nori. Top the bottom third of the rice with 3 teaspoons tuna mixture. To roll, lift the mat, compressing it against the filling as you roll the bottom edge in on itself. Continue rolling toward the top edge until only ¼ inch of the nori remains unrolled. Moisten your finger in the water, wet the edge of the nori, and press the mat to seal the roll. Set the roll aside, seam side down, and repeat.

3 With a sharp knife, slice each roll as preferred (see photo on page 30). Transfer to a platter and serve with the soy sauce, wasabi and pickled ginger.

This delicious roll features buttery smoked salmon and tart cucumber, a dynamite combo. Guests should make the salmon and cucumber logs before rolling.

SMOKED SALMON AND CUCUMBER MAKI

MAKES 8 ROLLS

8 large or 16 small slices smoked salmon, preferably tea-smoked

1 English cucumber, cut into ¼-by-8-inch strips, or as long as the nori

1 tablespoon rice vinegar mixed with 1 cup water, for rolling

8 cups Sushi Rice (opposite)

8 toasted nori sheets, halved lengthwise

Naturally brewed soy sauce

Wasabi

Sliced pickled ginger

1 Place 1 large or 2 small slightly overlapping slices of salmon on a work surface with a wide side near you. Place 2 cucumber strips a little above the near side of the salmon. Bring the near side of the salmon over the cucumber to enclose it, and roll to form a log. Transfer to a large plate and repeat.

2 To roll the sushi, have the vinegar-water mixture and sushi rice handy. Place 1 sheet of nori shiny side down on a sushi mat with one long edge toward you. With wet hands, pat 1 cup rice evenly over the bottom half of the nori. Place a salmon roll on the bottom third of the rice. Continue as in above recipe.

The almost creamy texture of avocado is one of the best things on the planet, I think. This simple but delicious roll features it, plus the flavors of lime, a touch of shallot, and togarashi, for heat.

AVOCADO-LIME MAKI

MAKES 8 ROLLS

2 ripe avocados, cut into long ¼-inch strips
Pinch of sea salt or kosher salt
1 to 3 pinches of togarashi, to taste
Juice of 1 lime
1 shallot, thinly sliced
16 shiso leaves (optional)
1 tablespoon rice vinegar mixed with 1 cup water, for rolling
8 cups Sushi Rice (page 32)
8 toasted nori sheets

Naturally brewed soy sauce
Wasabi
Sliced pickled ginger

1 Put the avocados in a medium bowl and season with the salt and togarashi. Add the lime juice and shallot and toss gently to avoid mashing the avocado.

2 To roll the sushi, have the vinegar-water mixture and sushi rice handy. Place 1 sheet of nori shiny side down on a sushi mat with one long edge toward you. With wet hands, pat 1 cup of the rice evenly over the bottom half of the nori.

3 Lay a few shallot slices, 2 shiso leaves, if using, and 3 or 4 of the avocado strips over the bottom third of the rice. To roll, lift the mat, compressing it against the filling as you roll the bottom edge in on itself. Continue rolling toward the top edge until only ¼ inch of the nori remains unrolled. Moisten your finger in the water-vinegar mixture, wet the edge of the nori, and press the mat to seal the roll. Set the roll aside, seam side down, and repeat with the remaining nori and filling.

4 With a sharp knife, slice each roll as preferred (see photo on page 30). Transfer the pieces to a platter and serve with the soy sauce, wasabi and pickled ginger.

This delicious roll features seared chicken breasts that have been rubbed with a spicy fennel-flavored mixture. If possible, have your guests prepare and cook the chicken, as the rolls are extra-super when the chicken in them is still hot.

FENNEL AND GARLIC CHICKEN MAKI

MAKES 8 ROLLS

1 tablespoon natural garlic powder

1 teaspoon cayenne or chile powder, or to taste

1 teaspoon paprika

1 tablespoon fennel seeds, crushed coarsely

½ cup all-purpose flour

2 bonless, skinless chicken breasts (about 1 pound), cut lengthwise into ¼-inch-thick strips

Kosher salt and freshly ground black pepper

2 large eggs

1 cup panko

2 tablespoons canola oil

1 bunch scallions, white and green parts, cut into 2-inch lengths

1 red bell pepper, cut into ¼-inch strips

1 tablespoon rice vinegar mixed with 1 cup water, for rolling

8 cups Sushi Rice (page 32)

8 toasted nori sheets

Naturally brewed soy sauce
Wasabi
Sliced pickled ginger

1 Line a large plate with paper towels. In a small bowl, combine the garlic powder, cayenne, paprika, fennel and flour. Transfer to a shallow dish. Season the chicken with salt and pepper.

2 Put the eggs and panko in two other shallow dishes. Beat the eggs with 1 tablespoon water until well combined. Dredge the chicken in the flour mixture, dip in the egg, drain the excess, and then dredge in the panko. Transfer to a plate.

3 Heat a medium skillet over medium heat. Add the oil and swirl to coat the pan. When the oil is hot, add the chicken and sauté, turning once, until golden and cooked through, 3 to 4 minutes per side. Transfer the chicken to the plate. Wipe out the pan, add the scallions and bell pepper, and sauté over medium-high heat until the vegetables have softened slightly, 2 to 3 minutes. Transfer to a plate.

4 To roll the sushi, have the vinegar-water mixture and sushi rice handy. Place 1 sheet of nori shiny side down on a sushi mat with one long edge toward you. With wet hands, pat 1 cup of the rice evenly over the bottom half of the nori.

5 Cover the rice with one-eighth of the chicken and top with one-eighth of the scallion mixture. To roll, lift the mat, compressing it against the filling as you roll the bottom edge in on itself. Continue rolling toward the top edge until only ¼ inch of the nori remains unrolled. Moisten your finger in the water, wet the edge of the nori, and press the mat to seal the roll. Set the roll aside, seam side down, and repeat with the remaining nori and filling.

6 With a sharp knife, slice each roll as preferred (see photo on page 30). Transfer to a platter and serve with the soy sauce, wasabi and pickled ginger.

This dish began with a near-disaster. I was making shumai for a Ty-Ku sake party, held in Aspen. As the guests were arriving I realized that the water I was going to cook the dumplings in wasn't going to boil at our high altitude. What to do? I grabbed a paella pan, put it on the grill, and added oil. I smashed—flattened—the shumai with a wet palm, then sautéed them until golden and crisp. The result, with its great textural play, was better than the original. These have a shrimp mousse filling that's deluxe but easy to do. They make a fantastic party nibble, but I think you'll want to serve them as a first course, too.

SMASHED SHRIMP SHUMAI

MAKES 20

1 pound medium shrimp, peeled and deveined

2 large eggs

½ cup (1 stick) unsalted butter, chilled and diced

1 teaspoon truffle oil (optional)

Kosher salt and freshly ground white pepper

16 thin square wonton wrappers

1 bunch scallions, white and green parts separated and thinly sliced, 2 tablespoons of the greens reserved for garnish

2 tablespoons sesame seeds

4 tablespoons canola oil

1 In a food processor, combine the shrimp and eggs and process until almost smooth. Add the butter and truffle oil, if using, season with salt and white pepper, and pulse until the butter is incorporated but still visible in small pieces. Test a small amount for seasoning by microwaving it at high power for 10 to 15 seconds, or by sautéing it in a little oil in a small pan. Adjust the seasoning if necessary. Use or place in a container, cover, and store refrigerated for up to 2 days.

2 To form the shumai, have a bowl of water handy. Hold 1 wonton wrapper in the palm of your non-dominant hand. Cup the hand and place 1 heaping tablespoon of the mousse in the center of the wrapper. Bring the wrapper up around the filling, pressing it to adhere to the filling and pleating as you go. Continue around the filling. There will be 6 to 8 pleats and the filling will be exposed. Tap the dumpling against the work surface to flatten the bottom. Repeat with the remaining wrappers and filling.

3 Put the scallions on a platter. Add the sesame seeds and combine. With a wet palm, press down on the shumai, flattening them to a thickness of about ½ inch. Press the "open" top side of the shumai into the scallion mixture.

4 Line a large plate with paper towels. Heat a large skillet over medium heat. Add 2 tablespoons of the oil and swirl to coat the pan. When the oil is hot, carefully add half the shumai to the pan coated side down and cook until golden, turning once, 1½ to 2 minutes per side. The tip of a paring knife, when inserted in the shumai, should emerge hot. Transfer the shumai to the paper towels to drain. Cook the remaining shumai with the remaining 2 tablespoons oil. Transfer to a platter, sprinkle with the reserved scallion greens, and serve.

To Drink:

A smooth, fruity white wine, like Teruzzi & Puthod Terre di Tufi, from Italy

I love halibut when it's perfectly cooked—and this recipe ensures just that. Enriched with olive oil and flavored with fennel, fresh halibut makes a luscious shumai filling. If you can find fennel pollen— yes, dried pollen from fennel plants—for the filling, by all means use it. It's intensely fennel-y *and* intriguingly sweet. These tempting dumplings are equally delicious as a party offering or first course.

STEAMED HALIBUT FENNEL SHUMAI

MAKES 24

1 tablespoon fennel pollen or
    fennel seeds

4 tablespoons extra-virgin olive oil

1 large onion, minced

1 large fennel bulb, halved, cored
    and diced, fronds reserved
    for garnish

Kosher salt and freshly ground
    black pepper

1 pound skinless halibut, preferably
    center-cut, cut into 1-inch chunks

2 large eggs

24 thin square wonton wrappers

1 If using fennel seeds, place them in a dry medium pan over medium heat and toast, tossing constantly, until just beginning to smoke lightly, 3 to 4 minutes. Immediately transfer the seeds to a rimmed plate and set aside.

2 Heat a large sauté pan over medium-high heat. Add 1 tablespoon of the oil and swirl to coat the pan. When the oil is hot, add the onion and fresh fennel and sauté, stirring, until the onion is caramelized, about 8 minutes. Season with salt and pepper and transfer to a medium bowl. Cool.

3 Meanwhile, in a food processor combine the halibut, eggs and remaining 2 tablespoons oil and pulse until well combined. Season with salt and pepper. Test a small amount for seasoning by microwaving it at high power for 10 to 15 seconds, or by sautéing it in a little oil in a small pan. Adjust the seasoning if necessary. Transfer the mousse to a medium bowl, add the fennel-onion mixture, and fold to combine.

4 To form the shumai, hold 1 wonton wrapper in the palm of your non-dominant hand. Cup the hand and place 1 heaping tablespoon of the mousse in the center of the wrapper. Bring the wrapper up around the filling, pressing it to adhere to the filling and pleating as you go. Continue around the filling. There will be 6 to 8 pleats and the filling will be exposed. Tap the dumpling against the work surface to flatten the bottom. Repeat with the remaining wrappers and filling.

5 Set up a steamer. If using a stainless-steel steamer, spray with nonstick cooking spray; if using a bamboo basket, line one or more compartments with a banana leaf, shredded cabbage, or parchment paper. When the water boils, working in batches if necessary, add the shumai to the steamer tray. Sprinkle the fennel pollen or toasted fennel seeds on the shumai. Steam until the filling is cooked through, or the tip of a paring knife inserted into the shumai comes out clean and feels hot, about 5 minutes.

To Drink:

A Chardonnay, like Montes Alpha

6 Transfer the shumai to a platter. Garnish with the fennel fronds and serve.

Everyone loves scallops and bacon. The salty smokiness of the bacon perfectly showcases the scallops' sweetness. Here, skewered, sautéed scallops are garnished with black bean mayo and crumbled bacon, a fabulous match-up. The scallops are threaded onto half skewers and make perfect, easily handled bites.

PAN-FRIED SCALLOP SATAYS
with Bacon and Black Bean Aioli

MAKES 12

36 bay scallops
6 thick slices bacon
1 tablespoon minced garlic
1 tablespoon chopped fermented
   black beans
1 bunch scallions, white and green
   parts separated, thinly sliced,
   1 tablespoon of the greens
   reserved for garnish
Kosher salt and freshly ground
   black pepper
2 egg yolks from large eggs, cold
1 tablespoon Dijon mustard
1 cup plus 1 tablespoon extra-virgin
   oil or more if needed
Juice of ½ lemon
Six 8-inch wooden skewers, or
   12 smaller ones

1 Using heavy kitchen shears, halve the 8-inch skewers, if using. Transfer to a bowl of water and soak for about 1 hour.

2 Skewer 3 scallops and arrange them near the top of each skewer. Refrigerate if not using immediately.

3 Meanwhile, cover a large plate with paper towels. Heat a large cast-iron skillet or sauté pan over medium-high heat, add the bacon and sauté, turning as needed, until crisp, about 4 minutes. Transfer to the paper towels to drain. Discard half the bacon fat from the pan. Chop the bacon and transfer to a dish.

4 Return the pan to medium heat. Add the garlic, black beans, and scallions and sauté, stirring, until the vegetables are soft, about 1 minute. Season with salt and pepper and transfer to a plate to cool. Wipe out the pan.

5 Make the mayonnaise: Place the egg yolks, mustard and 1 cup oil in a measuring pitcher and season with salt and pepper. Using an immersion blender, process until an emulsion forms, or prepare in a regular blender. Transfer the aioli to a small bowl and stir in the black bean mixture. Add the lemon juice and adjust the seasoning, if necessary. (If not serving right away, refrigerate.)

6 Season the scallops with salt and pepper. Heat the pan over medium-high heat, add the 1 tablespoon oil, and swirl to coat the pan. When the oil is hot, working in batches if necessary with additional oil, sauté the scallops, turning once, until just cooked through, 30 seconds per side. Transfer the scallops to a platter or plates, top with the aioli, garnish with the bacon and reserved scallion greens, and serve.

Ming's tips:

If you don't feel like making your own mayo, you can use a best-quality, canola oil–based brand.

If you can find small skewers, use them instead of halving the larger kind.

To Drink:

A white Rhone blend like JL Columbo Les Abeilles Côte de Rhone Blanc

It's amazing how popular goat cheese has become, and with reason. Besides its great taste, it's more healthful than many other natural cheeses. It also pairs beautifully with earthy shiitakes, as in these bites. The crostini are easily made and perfect for entertaining. I prefer to make them with a whole-wheat baguette, but feel free to use the regular kind, if you like.

SHIITAKE AND GOAT CHEESE CROSTINI

MAKES ABOUT 20

1 baguette, preferably whole wheat, sliced into ¼-inch rounds

2 tablespoons extra-virgin olive oil, plus more for brushing

Kosher salt and freshly ground black pepper

2 tablespoons minced garlic

8 ounces large shiitake mushrooms, stemmed and sliced ¼ inch thick

½ cup red wine

1 bunch chives, thinly sliced, a handful left whole for garnish

20 basil leaves

One (10-ounce) log goat cheese, cut into ¼-inch slices

1 Preheat the oven to 350°F. Place the bread rounds on a baking sheet, brush the tops with oil, and season lightly with salt and pepper. Bake, oiled side up, until golden, 10 to 12 minutes. Remove from the oven, flip the rounds and set aside. Turn the oven to broil.

2 Heat a large skillet over medium heat. Add 1 tablespoon of the oil and swirl to coat the pan. When the oil is hot, add the garlic and sauté, stirring, for 1 minute. Add the shiitakes, season with salt and pepper, and sauté, stirring, until softened, 2 to 3 minutes. Add the wine to deglaze the pan and allow the wine to evaporate, 1 to 2 minutes. Remove from the heat, add the chives, and stir to combine.

3 To make the crostini, top each bread round with a basil leaf, some of the shiitake mixture, and a slice of cheese. Drizzle with the remaining 1 tablespoon oil and season with pepper. Broil on the middle rack of the broiler just until the cheese becomes warm, 1½ to 2 minutes. Scatter the whole chives on a platter or plates, add the crostini, and serve immediately.

Ming's tip:

The easiest way to cut the cheese into rounds is to use a piece of fishing line or waxed unflavored dental floss, stretched taut. Alternatively, you can use a thin-bladed knife dipped into hot water.

To Drink:

A French Pinot Noir, like Arrogant Frog

I didn't invent the perfect combination of pears and gorgonzola, but their affinity did inspire the filling for these great "quesadillas." Another great party nibble, they're made with mu shu skins, whose thinness makes them more delicate than the usual tortilla-wrapped kind. The gorgonzola doesn't melt, so count it as a textural as well as a flavor element in the quesadillas. Spanish ham—you can also use proscuitto—adds class of its own.

GORGONZOLA AND GINGERED PEAR
"Quesadillas"

MAKES 8

4 just-ripe Bosc pears
Juice of 1 lime
1 tablespoon minced ginger
8 ounces gorgonzola cheese, crumbled
8 mu shu wrappers
8 thin slices Jamón ham or proscuitto
Canola oil

1 Peel, halve, and core the pears. Cut into ¼-inch dice, transfer to a medium bowl, and add the lime juice, ginger and gorgonzola. Stir gently.

2 Lay the wrappers flat on your work surface. Lay 1 or 2 slices of ham on the bottom half of each wrapper and top with the pear mixture. Fold the wrappers in half to make a half-moon shape.

3 Working in batches, and using 1 tablespoon oil for each, heat the oil in the pan over medium heat, swirling to coat the pan. When the oil is hot, carefully add as many quesadillas as will fit comfortably and cook until browned, about 2 minutes. With a large spatula, turn the quesadillas and brown the other side, about 2 minutes. Slice the quesadillas into 3 wedges each, transfer to a platter, and serve.

Ming's tip:
If you can't get mu shu wrappers, available at many Asian markets, you can use traditional flour tortillas instead.

Video tip:
Watch the video to see my simple technique for perfectly dicing pears.

To Drink:
A Pinot Grigio, like Kris or Alta Luna

As many people know, poke is a Hawaiian dish using cubed fish, raw or cooked. This cross-cultural poke, a simplified version of a Blue Ginger signature dish, features best-quality, stir-fried tuna cubes served on sushi rice in inexpensive Chinese spoons. People love this presentation, but you can use large tablespoons if you like, or eliminate the rice and serve the poke in a bowl as a "dip" with chips. You could also use salmon, halibut, or striped bass instead of the tuna, but whichever fish you choose, it must be top grade.

WOK-STIRRED TUNA POKE
on Sushi Rice

MAKES 30

1 tablespoon sesame seeds
2 bunches scallions, white and green parts separated, whites and half the greens cut into ¼-inch slices, the remaining greens thinly sliced
2 tablespoons minced ginger
¼ cup naturally brewed soy sauce
2 tablespoons honey
2 teaspoons toasted sesame oil
Freshly ground black pepper
1 pound center-cut big-eye or yellowfin tuna, cut into ½-inch dice
1 tablespoon canola oil
3 cups freshly cooked Sushi Rice (page 32)
Zest and juice of 1 lemon

30 Chinese spoons for serving

1 Put the sesame seeds in a dry wok over medium heat and toast, tossing constantly, until golden, about 30 seconds. Immediately transfer the seeds to a rimmed plate and set aside.

2 In a medium bowl, combine the scallion whites and the ¼-inch-sliced greens, the ginger, soy sauce, honey, and sesame oil. Season with pepper and stir. Add the tuna, stir gently, and transfer to the fridge to marinate for about 15 minutes. Drain the tuna of excess marinade.

3 Heat a wok or medium sauté pan over high heat. Add the oil and swirl to coat the pan. When the oil is hot, add the tuna and stir-fry until rare, about 1 minute, or longer if you prefer the tuna cooked through, about 3 minutes. Transfer to a plate.

4 Fill each spoon with a small quantity of rice. Top with the tuna and sprinkle with the lemon zest and juice. Garnish with the sesame seeds and thinly sliced scallion greens, and serve.

Ming's tip:

I give directions for toasting sesame seeds, but you can also buy them already toasted if you like.

Video tip:

Watch the video to learn tips for cutting the fresh tuna for best results.

To Drink:

A Champagne, like Saint Hilaire Blanc de Blanc

This is an awesome treatment of the usually humble parsnip. The vegetable is transformed into a suave purée that's garnished with curry-ginger oil and served in espresso cups, a festive presentation. The recipe makes enough purée to have on its own as a soup the next day; any leftover curry-ginger oil can be stored and used for making a deliciously spicy vinaigrette or for sautéing scallops, among other uses.

PARSNIP PURÉE
with Curry-Ginger Oil

MAKES 16

CURRY-GINGER OIL

¼ cup Madras curry powder

2 cups grapeseed or canola oil

¼ cup minced ginger

PARSNIP PURÉE

1 tablespoon canola oil

1 large onion, roughly chopped

Cloves from 1 head garlic, smashed with the flat of a knife

6 large parsnips, peeled and roughly chopped

Kosher salt and freshly ground black pepper

4 cups fresh chicken stock or low-sodium bought

2 tablespoons unsalted butter

2 tablespoons thinly sliced chives

1 Four hours in advance, or the day before, make the curry-ginger oil: In a large heavy saucepan, heat the curry powder over medium-high heat, stirring, until toasted, 30 seconds to 1 minute. Add the oil and heat. When the oil is hot, add the ginger and cook until it sizzles, about 30 seconds. Remove from the heat, allow the oil to cool slightly, then transfer to a glass jar. Allow the mixture to stand until the oil and curry powder have separated completely, about 4 hours. (Store in the refrigerator for at least 1 month if not using immediately.)

2 Make the parsnip purée: Heat a large soup pot over medium heat. Add the oil and swirl to coat the pan. When the oil is hot, add the onion and garlic and sauté, stirring, until caramelized, 3 to 4 minutes. Add the parsnips and sauté, stirring, for 2 minutes. Season with salt and pepper, add the stock, and bring to a simmer. Cook until the parsnips are tender and the liquid has reduced by one-third, 20 to 25 minutes. Working in batches if necessary, transfer to a blender and purée on the lowest speed. Add the butter and purée on high. Adjust the seasoning if necessary.

3 Transfer the purée to warmed espresso or other serving cups (see the Tip). Drizzle with the curry-ginger oil, garnish with the chives, and serve.

Ming's tip:

To heat the espresso cups for serving, put them in the sink and pour boiling water over them. Dry and use.

Video tip:

Watch the video for my simple roll-cutting technique for parsnips.

To Drink:

A Sonoma County Sauvignon Blanc, like Matanazas Creek

CHAPTER 2

Salads and Soups

When I think salads and soups, I think meals. Credit that to my French culinary training, which really introduced me to tantalizing main-dish salads and unique meal-in-one soups. Salads and soups, individually or together, make great lunches and dinners.

The salads here are all-occasion. Chicken Salad Chinoise, which pairs roast chicken with a tempting lettuce array, is perfect party fare. Miso-Shallot Shrimp Frisée Salad, an East-West blend that features miso-ponzu dressing; basil-

Salmon Salad with Shallot-Orange Vinaigrette all work perfectly for guests and family alike. Want to be the hit of someone else's party? Most of the salads can be prepared ahead for, say, pot-luck suppers, tossed with their vinaigrettes at the last minute and served.

Soups are meant to comfort. Quinoa and Tomato Soup starts with a beloved favorite—tomato soup—and includes the grain for hearty depth; Garlic-Ginger Sweet Potato Soup takes my favorite spud to a new and wonderfully satisfying height. I've tipped soups wholly into the rib-sticking zone with Chile Miso Pork Stew and Best 3-Meat Chile, which features ground turkey, pork and lamb, as well as black beans. Sambal Shrimp Gumbo, which also includes Chinese sausage, is a spicy "surf and turf" meal that's also great for company. And simplicity is key: All the soups are one-pot dishes, so they're easier on the cook. Whether soup or salad, the dishes here make the meal, in every sense.

This super salad, perfect for entertaining, was inspired by the popular chicken salad served by my friend Wolfgang Puck at his restaurant Chinois. My version offers two kinds of lettuce and shredded carrots as well as sliced cabbage, and features a light vinaigrette that balances hot Chinese mustard with a touch of honey. Added, too, are cashews and crisped chicken skin. I can't think of anything better to serve as the centerpiece of a summer meal—or, really, at any time of year when you want something light *and* satisfying.

CHICKEN SALAD CHINOISE

SERVES 4 TO 6

⅓ cup kosher salt for brining,
  plus more for seasoning
⅓ cup sugar
One 4- to 5-pound chicken
1 tablespoon canola oil
Freshly ground black pepper

VINAIGRETTE

1 large shallot, roughly chopped
2 tablespoons Dijon mustard
3 tablespoons Chinese hot mustard
  powder
¾ cup rice vinegar
1½ tablespoons naturally brewed
  soy sauce
3 tablespoons honey
2 tablespoons toasted sesame oil
Pinch of salt and freshly ground
  black pepper
¾ cup peanut or canola oil

1 head romaine lettuce, tough outer
  leaves removed, cored, halved,
  and cut widthwise into 1-inch
  pieces
½ small head Napa cabbage,
  quartered and thinly sliced
½ small head red cabbage, halved,
  cored and thinly sliced

1 Twelve to twenty-four hours in advance, brine the chicken: In a bowl large enough to hold the chicken and brine, combine the ⅓ cup salt, the sugar and 8 to 10 cups water. Stir to dissolve the salt and sugar, then add the chicken. If the chicken isn't covered, add more water. Refrigerate.

2 Preheat the oven to 500°F. Rinse the chicken well and pat dry inside and out. Coat inside and out with the 1 tablespoon canola oil, and season inside and out with salt and pepper. Place the chicken on a rack in a roasting pan breast side up and roast until brown, 15 to 25 minutes. Lower the oven temperature to 350°F and roast until cooked through, about 30 minutes, or until a meat thermometer inserted into the thickest part of the thigh reads 160°F. (Don't turn off the oven.) Transfer the chicken to a plate and, when cool enough to handle, remove the skin and transfer to a small baking dish. Pull the meat from the bones, tearing it into long shreds, season with salt and pepper, and set aside. Decrease the oven to 250°F, return the skin to the oven and roast until crisp, stirring occasionally, 10 to 12 minutes. Slice the skin into ¼-inch-wide strips, transfer to a plate and set aside.

3 Meanwhile, make the vinaigrette: In a blender combine the shallot, mustards, vinegar, soy sauce, honey and sesame oil, season with salt and pepper and blend until smooth. With the machine running, drizzle in the peanut oil. Taste and adjust the seasoning, if necessary.

4 In a large bowl, combine the romaine, cabbages, radicchio, carrots, scallion whites and jalapeños. Add the chicken, season with salt and pepper, add half of the vinaigrette, and toss. Add more vinaigrette, if necessary. Transfer to a platter and garnish with the chicken skin, nuts, and scallion greens. Arrange the lime quarters around the platter and serve.

1 head radicchio, halved, cored
 and thinly sliced
1½ cups shredded carrots
1 bunch scallions, white and
 green parts separated, sliced
 ¼ inch thick
1 jalapeño, minced
1 cup salted roasted cashews
2 limes, each cut into 6 wedges

To Drink:

A Pinot Gris, like Elk Cove

Ming's tips:

If you're in a hurry, buy already
roasted chicken from your market
or deli. If you can't get a large
chicken, buy smaller birds to equal
about 6 pounds.

At Blue Ginger we serve this
salad with an additional garnish
of fried wonton skins, which add
great crunch. To make them, cut
skins into ¼-inch strips, fry them in
canola oil that's heated to 350°F,
drain and salt them. Add with the
other garnishes.

Thai beef salad is an awesome blend of flavors and textures. There are many versions; mine combines the traditional rare grilled beef with a warm dressing made with chiles, fish sauce and lime juice, among other typical Thai ingredients. I westernize the dish, though, with the addition of carrots, cabbage and radicchio, whose soft crunch and slight bitterness are a terrific plus. I call for sirloin or strip steak to make this, but, really, you can use almost any cut. I've also had good luck with flank steak, which, besides being tasty, is easier on the pocketbook.

THAI BEEF SALAD

SERVES 4

6 tablespoons canola oil

One 10- to 12-ounce sirloin or strip steak, about 1 inch thick

Kosher salt and freshly ground black pepper

2 large shallots, minced

1 bunch scallions, white and green parts, thinly sliced, 1 tablespoon of the greens reserved for garnish

3 Thai bird chiles, or 2 serrano chiles, with seeds, minced

Juice of 3 limes

3 tablespoons fish sauce

1 small head white cabbage, cut into ⅛-inch slices

1 large or 2 small heads radicchio, cut into ¼-inch slices

2 large carrots, shredded

1 Heat a medium sauté pan or cast-iron skillet over medium-high heat. Add 2 tablespoons of the oil and swirl to coat the pan. Season the steak with salt and pepper and cook, turning once, until brown and medium-rare, 4 to 5 minutes per side. Set aside and let rest for 10 minutes.

2 Return the pan to medium heat. Add 1 tablespoon of the oil and swirl to coat the pan. When the oil is hot, add the shallots, scallions and chiles, season with salt and pepper, and sauté, stirring, until soft, about 1 minute. Remove from the heat, add the lime juice and fish sauce and whisk in the remaining 3 tablespoons canola oil.

3 In a large bowl, combine the cabbage, radicchio and carrots and toss with the warm vinaigrette. Adjust the seasoning, if necessary.

4 Slice the steak ¼ inch thick. Toss the steak and its juices with the salad, garnish with the reserved scallion greens and serve.

Ming's tip:

Save any extra slaw to serve the next day. The recipe yields 5 slices of beef per person. If you want beef with your leftover slaw, cook 2 steaks instead of 1.

Video tips:

Watch the video to learn the execution of a perfectly cooked steak, as well as the simple way to prep, slice and mince all the salad ingredients.

To Drink:

A chilled Gamay or a fruity wine like a Kermit Lynch Domaine Dupeuble Pere et Fils Beaujolais

When traveling in Japan in the 90s, I fell in love with a vinaigrette commonly served there. It features ponzu—the acidic note—plus shallots and miso. I think of miso as soy sauce on steroids; it gives an umami punch to all sorts of dishes, as it does to this warm shrimp salad. Included too are frisée and cherry tomatoes, great Western additions. You can cook the shrimp in advance, refrigerate them, and serve them in the salad cold, but I prefer them hot as then they help wilt the frisée.

MISO-SHALLOT SHRIMP FRISÉE SALAD

SERVES 4 TO 6

2 large shallots, roughly chopped
2 heaping tablespoons shiro miso
1 tablespoon wasabi powder mixed with 2 tablespoons room-temperature water
2 tablespoons shoyu ponzu
½ cup plus 1 tablespoon canola oil
Freshly ground black pepper
1 teaspoon toasted sesame oil
1 pound small (51-60) shrimp
Kosher salt
1 cup shredded carrots
2 heads frisée, cored, leaves torn, rinsed and dried
1 pint cherry tomatoes, halved

1 In a blender, combine the shallots, miso, wasabi and ponzu and blend at high speed. With the machine running, add 1 tablespoon water then gradually drizzle in the ½ cup oil. Season with salt and pepper, blend in the sesame oil and 2 to 4 tablespoons water, and set aside.

2 Heat a medium sauté pan over high heat. Add the remaining 1 tablespoon oil and swirl to coat the pan. When the oil is hot, add the shrimp, season with salt and pepper, and sauté, stirring, until the shrimp are cooked through, about 2 minutes.

3 In a large serving bowl, combine the carrots, frisée, tomatoes, and shrimp along with the juices and toss. Add enough vinaigrette to coat the salad lightly and toss. Taste to adjust the seasoning, toss, and serve.

Ming's tip:

The recipe yields more vinaigrette than you'll need. Save the extra to make a chicken salad dressing that's lighter than the usual mayo-based kind.

To Drink:

A Pinot Grigio, like Alta Luna, from Italy, or a Pinot Blanc

People should use cranberries more often. They're tarter than any other fruit and make a superior vinegar replacement in vinaigrettes. I use them in just that way in this great grilled chicken salad. The dressing, which also features grainy mustard and shallots, a classic French combo, pairs beautifully with the slight smokiness of the chicken. Served with crusty bread, this makes a great meal.

GRILLED CHICKEN SALAD
with Cranberry-Mustard Vinaigrette

SERVES 4 TO 6

⅓ cup kosher salt, for brining, plus more to season

⅓ cup sugar

4 boneless, skinless chicken breasts

Freshly ground black pepper

2 tablespoons canola oil, if grilling the chicken indoors

1 large or 2 small shallots, roughly chopped

2 tablespoons Pommerey mustard

1 cup cranberries

2 tablespoons naturally brewed soy sauce

1 cup extra-virgin olive oil

3 heads frisée, cored, leaves torn, rinsed and dried

1 pint cherry tomatoes, halved

1 The day before, brine the chicken: In a large pitcher, combine the ⅓ cup salt and the sugar with 8 cups water and stir to dissolve the sugar and salt. Place the chicken in a bowl or pot large enough to hold it and the brine, and pour the brine over the chicken. If the chicken isn't covered, make more brine and add it to the bowl. Refrigerate overnight. Rinse the chicken and pat dry.

2 Preheat an outdoor grill to high and lightly oil the grates. Season the chicken with salt and pepper and grill until just cooked through, turning once, 4 to 5 minutes per side. Alternatively, heat a large grill pan or cast-iron skillet over medium-high heat. Add the canola oil and swirl to coat the pan. When the oil is hot, add the breast and sauté, turning once, until cooked through, 4 to 5 minutes per side, or until the tip of a paring knife inserted in the thickest part of the meat feels hot when removed. Transfer the chicken to a cutting board, let rest for 5 minutes, then slice lengthwise into ¼-inch strips.

3 Meanwhile, in a blender, combine the shallots, mustard, cranberries, soy sauce and 2 tablespoons water, and blend on high speed until smooth. With the machine running, drizzle in the olive oil and season with salt and pepper.

4 In a large bowl, combine the chicken, frisée, tomatoes, and half the vinaigrette. Season with salt and pepper, and add more vinaigrette until lightly coated. Transfer the salad to serving plates, drizzle with additional vinaigrette, and serve.

To Drink:
A bright New World Sauvignon Blanc, like Isabel, from New Zealand

People who feel cheated when served a meatless main quickly embrace this salad. The flavors are vivid, and the crisp vegetables and succulent noodles contrast beautifully. A key to the dish's success is, interestingly, basil, which not only brightens the salad, but ties all the flavors together. Another key is wok-cooking. Considering my ancestry, I'm partial to the technique, but none other produces the vibrancy that characterizes this dish.

WOK-STIRRED VEGETABLES
and Rice Noodle Salad

SERVES 6

8 ounces rice stick noodles

1 tablespoon canola oil

1 tablespoon minced garlic

1 tablespoon minced ginger

1 bunch scallions, white and green parts separated, thinly sliced

½ head white cabbage, halved, cored and cut into ½-inch dice

Kosher salt and freshly ground black pepper

2 medium red bell peppers, cut into ½-inch dice

2 cups shredded carrots

4 tablespoons soy sauce

4 tablespoons rice vinegar

1 tablespoon sesame oil

½ cup packed basil leaves, cut into ¼-inch strips

1 Put the noodles in a large bowl and fill it with hot water to cover. When the noodles have softened, after about 15 minutes, drain, return to the bowl and set aside.

2 Heat a wok over medium-high heat. Add the oil and swirl to coat the pan. When the oil is hot, add the garlic, ginger and scallion whites and stir-fry until aromatic, about 30 seconds. Add the cabbage and stir-fry until wilted, about 1 minute. Season with salt and pepper, add the peppers and carrots, and toss. Add 2 tablespoons of the soy sauce and the vinegar, toss, remove from the heat, and adjust the seasoning with salt and pepper, if necessary.

3 Add half of the vegetables, the remaining 2 tablespoons soy sauce, the sesame oil and basil to the noodles. Mix well and season with salt and pepper.

4 Transfer the noodle mixture to a large serving platter, top with the remaining vegetables and garnish with the scallion greens. Serve immediately.

Video tips:

Watch the video to learn my simple technique for peeling and mincing ginger and the easy way to slice basil.

To Drink:

A Pinot Blanc, like Four Graces, from Oregon

Salmon must be the most popular fish in America. Besides being uniquely tasty, the fish has just the right fat content, and is delicious served hot, room temperature or cold. For this salad, I've paired salmon with a bright-tasting vinaigrette, whose dominant orange flavor, both tangy and sweet, complements and beings out the sweetness of the fish. With some bread, this makes a delicious light meal, and is really perfect for summer.

SALMON SALAD
with Shallot-Orange Vinaigrette

SERVES 4

½ cup pine nuts

1 pound skinless salmon, preferably center cut, cut into 1-inch cubes

Kosher salt and freshly ground black pepper

½ cup plus 1 tablespoon extra-virgin olive oil

1 large shallot, thinly sliced

2 tablespoons Dijon mustard

1 tablespoon minced ginger

8 ounces mesclun

4 oranges, juice and zest of 2, segments from 2

1 In a medium sauté pan, toast the pine nuts over medium-low heat, stirring constantly, until golden, 2 to 4 minutes. Transfer to a small bowl and set aside.

2 Season the salmon with salt and pepper. Add 1 tablespoon of the oil to the pan, and swirl to coat it. Heat the oil and when hot, add the salmon and sauté, stirring occasionally, until the salmon is medium-rare, 2 to 3 minutes, or 4 to 5 minutes for cooked through. Transfer the salmon to a large bowl.

3 In the container of an immersion blender, or in a regular blender, combine the shallot, mustard, ginger and orange juice. Season with salt and pepper and blend until the mixture is smooth. With the machine running, gradually drizzle in the ½ cup oil to make an emulsion.

4 In a large salad bowl, combine the mesclun, half the dressing and half the orange zest and segments. Season with salt and pepper and toss. The leaves should be lightly coated; add more dressing, if needed. Add the salmon and toss lightly. Garnish with the remaining zest and pine nuts and serve immediately.

Ming's tip:

To segment an orange easily, first cut off both ends deeply enough so you can see the flesh. Using the knife, peel the orange just close enough to the flesh so no pith remains. Trim away any remaining pith, if necessary. Working over a bowl to catch the juice, cut between the membranes that separate the segments, releasing them. Squeeze the membranes to get any remaining juice to use as you wish.

To Drink:

An unoaked Chardonnay, like La Crema, from California

If you were ever a kid, you undoubtedly had your share of canned tomato soup. It's a classic, but the soup's even better homemade. Heart- and soul-warming, my version features quinoa, which not only tastes great but, because it's a complete protein, is good for you. Ginger adds zing, and carrots lend sweetness. This is the kind of satisfying, stick-to-the-ribs dish that cold weather was made for.

QUINOA AND TOMATO SOUP

SERVES 8

3 tablespoons extra-virgin olive oil

2 large onions, roughly chopped

1 tablespoon minced ginger

2 large carrots, peeled and cut into ¼-inch rounds

4 ribs celery, thinly sliced

Kosher salt and coarsely ground black pepper

Two 28-ounce cans whole plum tomatoes

2 quarts fresh chicken stock or low-sodium bought

¼ cup wheat-free tamari

1 cup quinoa, rinsed

Parmesan for garnish

1 Heat a medium stock pot or soup pot over high heat. Add 2 tablespoons of the oil and swirl to coat the bottom. When the oil is hot, add the onions, ginger, carrots and celery, season with salt and pepper, and sauté, stirring every few minutes, until the vegetables are lightly caramelized, 10 to 12 minutes.

2 Add the tomatoes with their juice. Break them up and add the stock and tamari. Bring to a simmer and cook until the vegetables are soft, about 10 minutes.

3 With an immersion blender, or using a regular blender and working in batches, purée the soup. Add the quinoa, bring to a simmer, and cook until the quinoa is just tender, about 12 minutes.

4 Transfer the soup to individual soup bowls, grate Parmesan over each, and drizzle with the remaining tablespoon olive oil. Add a few grinds of pepper and serve.

Ming's tip:

This serves 8 amply; even so, you'll probably have leftover soup for another day.

To Drink:

Jasmine pearl or toasted rice green tea

I'm a soba noodle fanatic. In Japan, the noodles are often served as is with a dipping sauce of soy, dashi, and scallions. Why not, I wondered, use them in soup? Here's the result of my self-interrogation, a great soup, enhanced with sake, and served with a cool cucumber salad. This makes a great—and healthful—light lunch or first course.

SESAME SOBA NOODLE SOUP
with Cucumber Salad

SERVES 4

One 8- to 9-ounce package
  soba noodles
2 tablespoons canola oil
2 large onions, thinly sliced
Kosher salt and freshly ground
  black pepper
1 cup sake
3 tablespoons naturally brewed
  soy sauce
1 teaspoon toasted sesame oil
2 quarts fresh vegetable stock or
  low-sodium bought
1 heaping tablespoon wasabi
  powder mixed with 1 tablespoon
  room-temperature water
1 small English cucumber, very thinly
  sliced (see Tip)
1 tablespoon toasted sesame seeds

1 Fill a large bowl with water and add ice. In a medium stock pot or soup pot, cook the noodles in abundant salted water until al dente, about 7 minutes. Drain and transfer to the bowl. When the noodles are cold, drain well and set aside.

2 Return the pot to medium-high heat. Add 1 tablespoon of the canola oil and swirl to coat the bottom. When the oil is hot, add the onions, season with salt and pepper and sauté, stirring once, until caramelized, 10 to 12 minutes. Add the sake, and scrape the bottom of the pan to incorporate the brown bits, about 30 seconds. Add 2 tablespoons of the soy sauce, the sesame oil and stock and bring to a simmer. Add the noodles and heat through.

3 Meanwhile, in a medium bowl combine the wasabi, the remaining 1 tablespoon soy sauce, and the remaining 1 tablespoon canola oil. Add the cucumber, toss, and season with salt and pepper. Add half of the sesame seeds and toss.

4 Divide the soup among 4 soup plates. Make a mound of the noodles in each, top with the cucumber salad, garnish with the remaining sesame seeds and serve.

Ming's tip:

If you have a mandoline, use it to slice the cucumbers.

Video tip:

Watch the video to learn my trick for best cooling and draining the noodles.

To Drink:
Chilled Ty Ku Sake Black

My sweet potato jones goes back to childhood Thanksgivings, when they were served mashed and, yes, marshmallow-topped. My paternal grandfather, Yeh-Yeh, also loved the sweet potatoes, which, growing up, he bought hot from street vendors in China. This soup celebrates the sweet potato, boosted with garlic and ginger, its most complementary flavorings, I feel. This is everything you want from a soup—warming and good.

GARLIC-GINGER SWEET POTATO SOUP

SERVES 8

4 large sweet potatoes
1 tablespoon canola oil
2 large onions, cut into ¼-inch slices
2 tablespoons minced garlic
2 tablespoons minced ginger
1 jalapeño pepper, minced
Kosher salt and freshly ground
    black pepper
2 quarts fresh chicken stock or
    low-sodium bought
2 tablespoons naturally brewed
    soy sauce
2 tablespoons unsalted butter
    (optional)
2 tablespoons thinly sliced chives

1 Preheat the oven to 400°F. Wrap the sweet potatoes in foil, pierce them in several places with the point of a paring knife, and bake until a fork pierces them easily, about 45 minutes. When cool enough to handle, scoop the sweet potato flesh into a bowl and set aside.

2 Heat a stock pot or heavy soup pot over medium-high heat. Add the oil and swirl to coat the bottom. When the oil is hot, add the onions, garlic and ginger, season with salt and pepper and sauté, stirring, until softened, 3 to 4 minutes. Add the jalapeño and sauté, stirring, for 1 minute. Add the sweet potato, stock and soy sauce, taste to adjust the seasoning and bring to a simmer.

3 Using an immersion blender, purée the mixture. For a smoother texture, transfer the soup in batches to a regular blender or food processor and purée again. Alternatively, purée the mixture in batches in a blender only. With the blender running, add the butter, if using. Adjust the seasoning with salt and pepper. Divide the soup among serving bowls, garnish with the chives, and serve.

To Drink:

A lager, like Sam Adams

I first enjoyed pork stew in Santa Fe. It was made with Hatch green chiles, remarkable because their initial heat decrescendos to a lovely sweetness. They're difficult to find, though, and jalapeños work beautifully in the stew too. I include miso for the same reason I put it in other dishes—as a natural flavor enhancer. Added too are sweet potatoes and edamame for great textural contrast. Serve the stew with crusty whole-wheat bread and you're in business.

CHILE MISO PORK STEW

SERVES 6 TO 8

4 jalapeño peppers
3 green bell peppers
1 tablespoon paprika
1 tablespoon chile powder
1 tablespoon natural onion powder
1 tablespoon natural garlic powder
2 tablespoons kosher salt, plus additional for seasoning
2 pounds pork butt (shoulder), cut into 1-inch cubes
3 tablespoons canola oil, plus additional if needed
2 large onions, cut into 1-inch pieces
1 tablespoon minced garlic
Freshly ground black pepper
2 quarts fresh chicken stock or low-sodium bought
4 tablespoons shiro miso
2 large sweet potatoes, peeled and cut into ½-inch dice
2 cups shelled edamame
Crusty bread

1 Turn a gas burner to high. Skewer the jalapeños on a metal skewer and place on the burner. Allow the peppers to bubble and turn black, 2 to 3 minutes. When one side is charred, protecting your fingers with a potholder or kitchen towel, turn the skewer and char the peppers on the second side, 2 to 3 minutes. Alternatively, char the peppers under the broiler. Transfer to a brown paper bag, close the bag and let sit to steam for 5 or 10 minutes. This helps loosen the skin. Remove the peppers from the bag, and with your fingers or a damp paper towel, rub off the skin. Remove and discard the stem, seeds, and veins. Repeat the procedure with the bell peppers, turning them with tongs until they're blistered on all sides. Cut the peppers into 1-inch pieces and transfer them and the chiles to a plate. Set aside.

2 In a medium bowl, combine the paprika and the chile, onion and garlic powders. Add the 2 tablespoons salt and mix well. Add the pork, toss to coat it well, and transfer to the refrigerator to flavor for at least 1 hour or overnight.

3 Heat a small stock pot or heavy soup pot over medium-high heat. Add 1 tablespoon the oil and swirl to coat the bottom. Add half the pork and brown on all sides, 4 to 5 minutes. Transfer the pork to a plate and set aside. Repeat with another tablespoon of oil and the remaining pork.

4 Wipe out the pot and heat over medium-high heat and add the remaining 1 tablespoon oil. Swirl to coat the bottom and when the oil is hot, add the onions and garlic and sauté, stirring, until browned, 5 to 6 minutes. Add the peeled peppers, return the pork to the pot. Add the stock and bring to a simmer. Place the miso in a strainer, dip it into the stock, and whisk to dissolve the miso into the soup. Adjust the seasoning with salt and pepper and simmer until the pork is tender, about 1½ hours.

5 Add the sweet potatoes and edamame and simmer until the sweet potatoes are tender, 15 to 20 minutes. Transfer to individual bowls and serve with the bread.

To Drink:

A lager, like Yanjing, or an off-dry Riesling, like Leitz "Eins Zwei Dry"

Ming's tips:

If you can find Hatch green chiles, fresh, frozen, or canned, use 2 cups chopped instead of the jalapeños. If using the canned kind, drain the chiles first.

You can make this dish in a pressure cooker to save time. Follow the instructions up to the final simmering and lock the lid in place according to the manufacturer's instructions. When the steam begins to hiss out of the cooker, reduce the heat to low, just enough to maintain a very weak whistle, and cook for 30 minutes. Release the pressure, add the potatoes and edamames, lock on the lid, and cook for another 15 minutes.

Everyone loves chili. This super version contains ground turkey, pork and lamb, plus black beans. It's also easy to cook and satisfies everybody, kids included. I usually pass cornbread with this, but sometimes I'm tempted to serve it as the Skyline Diner in Dayton, Ohio, served its chili when I was growing up—on pasta. Why not?

BEST 3-MEAT CHILI

SERVES 6 TO 8

2 tablespoons canola oil
2 large onions, cut into ½-inch dice
2 tablespoons thinly sliced garlic
3 jalapeño peppers, 2 minced, and
　1 cut into thin rings for garnish
Kosher salt and freshly ground
　black pepper
2 tablespoons paprika
2 tablespoons chile powder
2 tablespoons ground ginger
1 pound ground turkey
1 pound ground pork
1 pound ground lamb
One 28-ounce can diced tomatoes
One 16-ounce can black beans,
　drained
1 cup shelled edamame
4 tablespoons naturally brewed
　soy sauce
1 quart fresh chicken stock or low-
　sodium bought, or as needed
1 to 2 cups cooked 50-50 White and
　Brown Rice (optional;
　page 13)
1 cup plain Greek yogurt
½ cup chopped cilantro

1 Heat a large casserole or Dutch oven over medium-high heat. Add the oil and swirl to coat the bottom. When the oil is hot, add the onions, garlic and minced jalapeños, season with salt and pepper and sauté, stirring, until the onions are lightly colored, about 6 minutes.

2 Add the paprika, chile powder and ground ginger. Season with salt and pepper and sauté, stirring, for 30 seconds. Add the three ground meats, season with salt and pepper, and sauté, breaking it up, about 2 minutes. Add the tomatoes with their juice, and stir, scraping the bottom of the pot to incorporate any browned bits. Add the black beans, edamame, soy sauce and enough stock to cover the meat. Add the rice, if using, to thicken to the degree preferred and simmer until the chili is reduced by one-quarter, about 30 minutes, or 1 hour, if not using rice. Adjust the seasoning with salt and pepper.

3 Transfer the chili to individual serving bowls. Garnish with the yogurt, cilantro and jalapeño rings and serve.

Ming's tip:
This dish makes enough chili to store and serve on another day.

To Drink:
A beer like Dogfish Head
60 Minute IPA

This "Nawleens" specialty has many versions. My favorite ones, though, include "surf and turf," seafood and meat like ham or sausage. This version features shrimp and Chinese sausage or bacon, but in place of the usual flour- and oil-based roux thickening, I use a cornstarch slurry, which makes a lighter dish that's also gluten-free. Another bow to the East, besides the sausage, is the sambal, which gives the gumbo real kick. There's okra in it too, which couldn't be more traditional. Served with cornbread, as I like to do, this is a terrific full-meal dish that's particularly great for company.

SAMBAL SHRIMP GUMBO

SERVES 6 TO 8

1 tablespoon canola oil

4 Chinese sausages, sliced
¼ inch thick; or 4 slices bacon,
cut ¼-inch thick

1 tablespoon minced garlic

2 large onions, minced

Kosher salt and freshly ground
black pepper

1 head celery, ribs cut into
¼-inch slices

2 large bell peppers, red and
green, minced

1 tablespoon paprika

2 tablespoons sambal or hot sauce

4 tablespoons organic
Worcestershire sauce

1 pound okra, stemmed and cut into
½-inch slices

2 quarts fresh chicken stock or
low-sodium bought

2 tablespoons cornstarch mixed with
2 tablespoons water

2 pounds small (51–60) shrimp

6 to 8 cups 50-50 White and Brown
Rice (page 13), for serving

1 Heat a large casserole or Dutch oven over medium-high heat. Add the oil and swirl to coat the bottom. When the oil is hot, add the sausages and cook until their fat is rendered, 1 to 2 minutes. If using bacon, cook it until crisp, 3 to 4 minutes.

2 Add the garlic and onions, season with salt and black pepper, and sauté, stirring, until translucent, about 2 minutes. Add the celery, bell peppers and paprika, adjust the seasoning with salt and pepper, and sauté, stirring, until tender, 2 to 3 minutes. Add the sambal and Worcestershire sauce, and sauté, stirring, for 1 minute. Add the okra, stir, and season with salt. Add the stock, adjust the seasoning, bring to a simmer, covered, and cook until the mixture is reduced by a fifth, about 10 minutes.

3 Whisk in the slurry, add the shrimp, return to a simmer and cook until cooked through, about 2 minutes. Adjust the seasoning with salt and pepper.

4 Divide the rice among soup plates. Top with the gumbo and serve.

Video tip:

Watch the video to learn all about okra.

To Drink:

A Pinot Gris, like Trimbach Reserve
Personnelle

CHAPTER 3

Seafood

Seafood invites invention. It's a great canvas for many flavoring approaches. Glazes and marinades, to name two, flavor seafood deliciously with little work for the cook.

Take Soy-Sake Salmon with Almond Fried Rice, an update of trout almondine that's powered by the fish's preliminary bath in soy sauce, sake, honey and lime juice. Ginger-Citrus Swordfish with Fennel Salad benefits similarly from an orange-lemon marinade, which is also cooked and used to dress the accompanying salad. Broiled Miso-Glazed Salmon with Lime-Cucumber Orzo is glazed with a miso mixture that yields a complementary sweetness and irresistibly crisp, caramelized skin.

Succulent, quick-cooking shrimp are similarly flavor-friendly. Spicy Shrimp with Mango and Rice Noodles contrast sambal heat, mango sweetness, and chewy noodles for truly exciting eating. Tempura Shrimp with Avocado and Ponzu Dipping Sauce not only delivers the best tempura shrimp ever, but accompanies it with buttery-crisp tempura avocado.

Seafood is also great for entertaining. Thai Seafood Noodle Pot, a meal-in-one featuring clams, mussels, and rice vermicelli, is an elbows-on-the table treat, while Banana Leaf–Wrapped Chile Halibut—the fish is cooked in packages that are opened at table—makes any dinner party deluxe. Buy the most pristine seafood you can get, flavor it imaginatively, cook it to perfect doneness—I show you how—and seafood makes the meal.

I had my first trout almondine in the only French restaurant in Dayton, Ohio, my hometown. I loved the contrast of the crunchy almonds and buttery fish. I honor that classic combo of fish and almonds in this recipe, but use salmon, a richer, more luscious fish, instead of trout. The salmon gets a piquant sweet-sour marinade that's also used to make a pan sauce. The almonds go into the rice, which also includes scallions and scrambled eggs. This is a homey dish that's also great for casual entertaining.

SOY-SAKE SALMON
with Almond Fried Rice

SERVES 4

Four 6-ounce skinless center-cut
  salmon fillets
½ cup plus 1 tablespoon naturally
  brewed soy sauce
½ cup sake
2 tablespoons honey
Juice from 2 limes
1 cup slivered almonds
3 large eggs
Kosher salt and freshly ground
  black pepper
6 tablespoons canola oil
1 tablespoon minced ginger
2 bunches scallions, white and green
  parts, sliced ¼ inch thick,
  1 tablespoon of the greens
  reserved
6 cups cooked and cooled jasmine
  or basmati rice or other long-grain
  rice (see Tip, page 13)
2 tablespoons unsalted butter

To Drink:

A chilled Sake, like Ty Ku Black,
or a crisp Chardonnay, like Eric
Chevalier, from France

1 Put the salmon in a deep plate. In a small bowl, combine the ½ cup soy sauce, sake, honey and lime juice. Pour over the salmon and marinate for at least 15 minutes and up to 1 hour.

2 In a wok, toast the almonds over medium heat, stirring constantly, until golden, 3 to 5 minutes. Transfer to a small bowl and set aside.

3 Line a large plate with paper towels. In a small bowl, beat the eggs and season with salt and pepper.

4 Heat the wok over high heat. Add 4 tablespoons of the oil and swirl to coat the pan. When the oil is almost smoking, add the eggs, which will puff. Stir to scramble, about 10 seconds, and transfer to the paper towels to drain.

5 Reduce the heat to medium-high. Add 1 tablespoon of the oil to the pan and swirl to coat the pan. Add the ginger and scallions and sauté, stirring, for about 30 seconds. Season with salt and pepper, add the rice, almonds, eggs and remaining 1 tablespoon soy sauce, and stir to blend, breaking up the eggs. Adjust the seasoning, if necessary, and transfer to a large bowl.

6 Remove the salmon from the marinade and pat dry. Reserve the marinade.

7 Heat a large sauté pan over medium-high heat. Add the remaining tablespoon oil and swirl to coat the bottom. When the oil is hot, add the salmon nicest side down and cook until golden, about 1 minute. Flip the salmon, lower the heat to medium-low and cook for 2 minutes. Increase the heat to medium and turn the salmon on one edge and cook for 2 minutes more. Turn onto the remaining edge and cook until medium, 2 minutes more. Transfer to a plate.

8 Wipe out the pan. Add the marinade and bring to a simmer over medium heat. Add the reserved scallions and reduce the marinade by half, 1 to 2 minutes. Remove from the heat and whisk in the butter. Taste to adjust the seasoning.

9 Spread the rice on a platter or divide it among individual plates and top with the salmon. Drizzle the fish with the pan sauce and serve.

Ming's tip:

If you get tail-end fillets, sauté them on 2 sides only, not on their edges.

I'm so happy that swordfish is available again after a decade of being overfished. The key to making the best of this wonderful fish is to marinate it first in a tenderizing bath that contains an acid—here, orange and lemon juices. Nothing goes better with citrus than soy sauce, and that's in the marinade too. Fennel, a vegetable I love, accompanies the fish—it's also a sucker for citrus, so the whole dish is deliciously harmonious. This is an all-season entrée—light enough for summer, but also great in winter when citrus fruit is at its best.

GINGER-CITRUS SWORDFISH
with Fennel Salad

SERVES 4

2 large fennel bulbs, halved, cored, and shaved (see Tip), fronds reserved for garnish

4 large oranges, juice of 2, the others segmented, 7 segments reserved for garnish

Juice of 1 lemon

1 tablespoon naturally brewed soy sauce

1 tablespoon minced ginger

1½ pounds skinless swordfish steak, preferably center cut, bloodline removed, cut into eight 1-by-1-inch logs

Kosher salt and freshly ground black pepper

2 tablespoons fennel seeds, crushed

4 tablespoons extra-virgin olive oil

1 Put the shaved fennel in a large bowl. Set aside.

2 In a medium bowl, combine the orange and lemon juices, soy sauce and ginger until blended. Add the swordfish, turn gently to coat, and marinate for 10 minutes.

3 Transfer the fish to a large plate and pat dry. Season with salt and pepper and sprinkle evenly with the fennel seeds. Reserve the marinade.

4 Heat a large sauté pan over medium heat. Add 1 tablespoon of the oil and swirl to coat the pan. When the oil is hot, add the fish and sauté on all sides until it is almost cooked through, 1 to 2 minutes minute per side. Transfer the fish to a plate.

5 Put the marinade in a small saucepan and bring to a simmer over medium-high heat. Whisk in the remaining 3 tablespoons oil and season with salt and pepper. Add all but the reserved orange segments to the bowl with the fennel. Add 4 tablespoons of the marinade, toss and season with salt and pepper.

6 Divide the fennel salad among serving plates. Top with the swordfish and drizzle with the remaining marinade. Garnish with the fennel fronds and orange segments and serve.

To Drink:

A bright New World Sauvignon Blanc, like Dog Point Vineyard, from New Zealand

Ming's tip:

A mandoline makes shaving the fennel a breeze. Kyocera makes an inexpensive one that works like a charm.

Video tip:

Watch the video to learn how to select the freshest swordfish and properly prepare it.

The combination of hot and sweet is famously exciting and gets full play here with sambal-spiced shrimp and luscious mango. The mango brings out the shrimps' sweetness and vice versa. Rice noodles, like tofu, are remarkable flavor-carriers, and thus ensure a super-tasty dish; they're also delightfully chewy. This is great for a simple weeknight supper, but you'll enjoy it as a weekend lunch, too.

SPICY SHRIMP WITH MANGO
and Rice Noodles

SERVES 4

1 pound snow peas
Kosher salt
1 package (about 9 ounces) rice sticks
3 tablespoons canola oil
1 tablespoon minced ginger
1 bunch scallions, white and green parts, thinly sliced, 1 tablespoon of the greens reserved for garnish
Freshly ground black pepper
1 pound small (51–60) shrimp
1 tablespoon sambal or other hot sauce
2 mangos, peeled and cut into ½-inch pieces
1 cup fresh chicken stock or low-sodium bought
1 tablespoon rice vinegar or lemon juice

1 Fill a large bowl with water and add ice cubes. Blanch the peas in abundant salted water until bright green, about 45 seconds. Drain the peas and transfer to the ice water. Transfer the cooking water to a large bowl. When the peas are cold, drain them and pat dry. Set aside.

2 Add the noodles to the bowl with the cooking water. (If the noodles aren't submerged, add hot water.) When the noodles have softened, after about 15 minutes, drain and set aside.

3 Heat a wok or large sauté pan over medium-high heat. Add 2 tablespoons of the oil and swirl to coat the pan. When the oil is hot, add the ginger and all but the reserved scallions. Season with salt and pepper and sauté, stirring, until aromatic, 30 seconds to 1 minute. Add the shrimp and sauté, stirring, until the shrimp are almost cooked through, about 2 minutes. Season with salt and pepper, add the sambal and mangos, and sauté until the shrimp are cooked through, about 1 minute. Add the snow peas, noodles and stock and simmer, tossing, until the liquid is reduced by three-quarters, 3 to 4 minutes. Add the vinegar and season with salt and pepper. Transfer to a platter, garnish with the reserved scallion greens, and serve.

To Drink:
A Riesling, like Hugel, from Alsace

Steaming noodle pots—meal-in-one dishes that contain noodles and other fresh ingredients—are a Southeast Asian staple. My Thai-influenced version features mussels and clams plus rice vermicelli for great texture. Shellfish retain all their flavor when cooked in broth, as here, and the taste-combo of chile heat, fish sauce, lime juice and shallots is winning, to say the least. This is quickly done and couldn't be more welcome for cold-weather dining.

THAI SEAFOOD NOODLE POT

SERVES 4

¼ cup cornmeal

1 pound littleneck or other small clams

1 package (about 9 ounces) rice vermicelli

1 tablespoon canola oil

3 large shallots, thinly sliced

2 fresh Thai bird chiles or 1 jalapeño, thinly sliced

Six 3-by-¼-inch-thick slices ginger

Kosher salt and freshly ground black pepper

1 pound mussels, preferably Prince Edward Island, scrubbed

1 cup white wine

6 cups fresh chicken stock or low-sodium bought, or vegetable stock

2 tablespoons fish sauce

Juice of 2 limes

1 pound small (51–60) shrimp, peeled and deveined

Leaves from ½ bunch Thai or regular basil, plus additional for garnish

1 Fill a large bowl with water. Add the cornmeal, stir, and add the clams. Let the clams purge for at least 1 hour and up to 3. Rinse, drain the clams well, and set aside. Discard the water and cornmeal.

2 Put the noodles in a large bowl and fill it with hot water to cover. When the noodles have softened, after about 15 minutes, drain and set aside.

3 Heat a stock pot or wok over high heat. Add the oil and swirl to coat the bottom. When the oil is hot, add the shallots, chiles and ginger and sauté, stirring, until fragrant, about 30 seconds. Season with salt and pepper. Add the clams, toss, and cook until the clams start to open, about 4 minutes. Add the mussels and wine, toss, and cook until the wine is reduced by half, about 1 minute. Add the stock, stir in the fish sauce, and add half of the lime juice. Adjust the seasoning with salt and pepper, cover, and cook until the shellfish have opened, 5 to 6 minutes, or less if the clams are small. Add the noodles, shrimp, and basil and bring to a simmer. Cover and cook until the shrimp are cooked through, 2 to 3 minutes, remove from the heat, adjust the seasoning with salt and pepper, and add the remaining lime juice. (Discard any unopened shellfish.) Transfer to a large serving bowl, garnish with the basil and serve.

Video tip:

Watch the video to learn about prepping clams and mussels.

To Drink:

An off-dry Chenin Blanc, like Remy Pannier Vouvray

Is there anything better than crisp tempura shrimp? My version is particularly delicate, thanks to a batter made from rice flour, club soda and beer, which adds a pleasingly yeasty taste and ups the crispness ante. If you've never had tempura avocado, you haven't lived. Its rich, buttery flesh is a perfect foil for its crisp exterior. Add ponzu dipping sauce and you're in for seriously great eating.

TEMPURA SHRIMP WITH AVOCADO
and Ponzu Dipping Sauce

SERVES 4 TO 6

2 cups rice flour
1 teaspoon togarashi or cayenne, or to taste
⅔ cup club soda, or more if needed
½ cup beer, or more if needed
1 bunch scallions, white and green parts separated, thinly sliced
Canola oil for frying
12 large (U-15) shrimp, peeled, deveined, and butterflied (see Tip)
Kosher salt
2 ripe-firm avocados, halved, each half cut into 3 wedges
1 cup ponzu
1 tablespoon minced ginger

1 Put the rice flour and togarashi in a large bowl and whisk in the soda and beer gradually until the mixture has the consistency of pancake batter. Stir in the scallion whites and half the greens. Set aside.

2 Line a large plate with paper towels. Fill a deep stock pot or Dutch oven one-third full with oil and heat over medium-high heat. When the oil is 350°F, and working in batches of 4 or 5, dip the shrimp into the batter, shake off any excess, and add to the oil. Fry until the shrimp are golden, 2 to 3 minutes. With a skimmer, transfer the shrimp to the paper towels to drain. Season with salt and transfer to a serving platter.

3 Return the oil to 350°F. Dip the avocado into the batter, drain, and fry until golden, 2 to 3 minutes. Transfer to the paper towels to drain. Salt.

4 Meanwhile, in a medium serving bowl, combine the ponzu, ginger and the remaining scallion greens. Arrange the shrimp on a platter, surround with the avocado, and serve immediately with the dipping sauce on the side.

Ming's tips:

To butterfly the shrimp, after deveining, place the shrimp on a flat surface and slice carefully across the open side toward but not through the side opposite. Unfold the shrimp, pressing it gently against your work surface.

If you don't have a frying thermometer, you can tell when the oil is hot enough for frying by dribbling a bit of batter from the end of a chopstick into it. If the batter puffs up and floats, the oil is ready.

You can fry the shrimp and avocado together, in batches, rather than individually.

To Drink:

A sparkling rosé, like Je T'aime Brut Rose, or beer, like Yanjing

I love this dish of crisp caramelized salmon paired with sprightly lime-flavored orzo. Miso, the basis of the glaze, has to be one of my favorite ingredients—it's packed with flavor. But its natural saltiness needs to be toned down, and that's just what sake, also used in the glaze, does here. The light and freshly acidic orzo balances the richness of the fish for a marriage made in—well, you know.

BROILED MISO-GLAZED SALMON
with Lime-Cucumber Orzo

SERVES 4

⅓ cup shiro miso
3 tablespoons honey
¾ cup sake
⅓ cup canola oil, plus 1 tablespoon
  if needed
Four 6- to 7-ounce salmon fillets,
  preferably center cut, skin on
Kosher salt
1½ cups orzo, preferably
  whole wheat
2 tablespoons extra-virgin olive oil
1 large English cucumber, diced
1 bunch scallions, white and green
  parts, sliced ¼ inch thick
Juice of 2 limes
Freshly ground black pepper

1 In a blender, combine the miso, honey and sake and blend. With the machine running, drizzle in the ⅓ cup canola oil and blend until the mixture is emulsified. Put the salmon in a small nonreactive bowl, pour the marinade over it, spooning the marinade under and around the fillets to make sure they're evenly coated. Cover with plastic wrap and refrigerate for 12 to 24 hours, turning once or twice.

2 Place an oven rack in the middle position and preheat the broiler. Fill a large bowl with water and add ice cubes. In a large pot, cook the pasta in abundant salted water until al dente, about 7 minutes; drain and add to the ice water. When the pasta is cold, drain the pasta. Return the pasta to the bowl, and toss with 1 tablespoon of the olive oil. Add the cucumber, scallions, lime juice and remaining 1 tablespoon olive oil. Season with salt and pepper, toss, and set aside.

3 Remove the salmon from the marinade and place it on paper towels to drain. Season the skin side with pepper. Preheat a large ovenproof sauté pan in the oven until very hot, about 10 minutes. Remove and spray with nonstick cooking spray or brush with 1 tablespoon canola oil. Add the salmon skin side up, transfer to the middle rack of the broiler, and broil for 7 minutes for medium, 10 minutes for well-done. For very crisp skin, transfer the salmon to the top rack and broil, watching carefully to avoid burning, 15 to 30 seconds. Transfer the orzo to a platter or divide among 4 individual plates. Top with the salmon, skin side up, and serve.

To Drink:
A Chardonnay, like A to Z, from
Oregon or Ty Ku Sake Black

The best food I've enjoyed in Singapore is sold in seafood stalls. Their chile-fired skate in banana leaves is dynamite in more ways than one. Here's my version, which replaces hard-to-get skate with delicious halibut. The fish is chile-seasoned and wrapped in the leaves—or in paper and foil, if you wish—and baked. The packages are opened at the table, where they release super-fragrant steam. Talk about aromatherapy!

BANANA LEAF-WRAPPED CHILE HALIBUT

SERVES 4

2 tablespoons canola oil

2 red jalapeño peppers, minced (see Tip)

1 tablespoon minced ginger

2 red onions, diced

1 teaspoon paprika

2 tablespoons fish sauce

2 limes, 1 juiced, the other cut into 4 wedges

Kosher salt and freshly ground black pepper

4 banana leaves

Four 6-ounce halibut fillets, preferably center-cut

To Drink:

A Gewürztraminer, like Chateau Ste. Michelle

Ming's tip:

I call for red jalapeños, which are slightly hotter than the green, but you can certainly use the regular kind.

1 Preheat the oven to 400°F.

2 Heat a large ovenproof sauté pan over medium-high heat. Add 1 tablespoon of the oil and swirl to coat the pan. When the oil is hot, add the jalapeños, ginger and onions and sauté, stirring, until the onions are soft, about 4 minutes. Add the paprika, stir, and add the fish sauce. Remove the pan from the heat and add the lime juice. Toss, season with salt and pepper, and transfer to a medium bowl. If using banana leaves, wipe out the sauté pan and set aside.

3 Place a banana leaf on your work surface with a wide side near you. Alternatively, cut 4 sheets each of parchment paper and foil about 12-by-12 inches and place one banana leaf or sheet of paper on your work surface. Smear one-eighth of the chile mixture on the center of the leaf or sheet and place one of the halibut pieces, nicest side up, in the center of the leaf or paper with the widest side parallel to the wide side of the wrapper. Season with salt and pepper and smear with another eighth of the chile mixture. Bring the near side of the wrapper over the fish, then fold the far side over the first. Turn in the sides to enclose the fish completely. If using a banana leaf, secure the package with butcher's twine; if using paper, wrap the package in the foil and close to seal. Repeat with the remaining chile mixture and pieces of fish.

4 If using banana leaves, heat the sauté pan over medium heat. Add the remaining 1 tablespoon oil and swirl to coat the pan. When the oil is hot, add the fish, nicer side down, and sauté until the leaf browns slightly, about I minute. If using parchment and foil, skip this step, and transfer the packages to the pan. Transfer to the oven and bake until the fish is just cooked through, 8 to 10 minutes. Test by inserting the tip of a paring knife into the fish for 3 seconds; if it emerges hot, the fish is done. Alternatively, a thermometer inserted into the fish will read 130°F.

5 Cut the twine from the packages or remove the foil. Transfer the packages to plates, folded side down if wrapped in banana leaves, and open the packages at the table with sharp scissors. Serve with the lime wedges on the side.

Having lived in New England for more than twenty years, I've had my share of cod. It's an unassuming fish, but one with great texture and subtle flavor. Here, the fish is coated in scallion-flavored panko, fried until golden, and served on red onions and chard. Chard is an underused vegetable—I think of it as a cross between spinach and kale—that when properly cooked, as here, brings raves.

SCALLION-PANKO COD
with Red Onions and Swiss Chard

SERVES 4

1 cup all-purpose flour

3 large eggs

2 cups panko

1 heaping teaspoon ground white pepper

1 heaping teaspoon natural garlic powder

2 bunches scallions, white and green parts separated, thinly sliced

Four 6-ounce cod fillets

Kosher salt and freshly ground black pepper

4 tablespoons extra-virgin olive oil

2 red onions, thinly sliced

1 tablespoon minced ginger

1 bunch Swiss chard, bottom stems cut away, leaves cut into ¼-inch ribbons

Juice and zest of 1 lemon, plus lemon slices for garnish

1 Preheat the oven to 350°F. Put the flour, eggs and panko in separate shallow dishes. Add the white pepper and garlic powder to the flour and blend. Beat the eggs with 2 tablespoons water until well combined. Add all but 3 tablespoons of the scallion greens to the panko and stir to mix.

2 Dry the cod with paper towels and season with salt and pepper. Dredge the cod in the flour, dip in the egg, drain excess, then dredge in the panko mixture. Transfer to a large plate.

3 Heat a large ovenproof sauté pan over medium-high heat. Add 2 tablespoons of the oil and swirl to coat the pan. When the oil is hot, add the fish and sauté, turning once, until golden, about 1 minute per side. Transfer to a large plate and set aside.

4 Wipe out the pan, add 1 tablespoon oil, and swirl to coat the pan. When the oil is hot, add the scallion whites, onions and ginger and sauté, stirring, until the onions are soft, about 2 minutes. Add the chard stems and sauté for 30 seconds, stirring, then add the leaves. Season with salt and pepper, add the lemon juice and zest and sauté, stirring, until the chard has started to soften, about 1 minute. Top with the fish, transfer to the oven and bake until the fish is just cooked through, with an internal temperature of 130°F, 10 to 12 minutes. Transfer the chard to serving plates and top with the cod. Drizzle with the remaining 1 tablespoon oil, garnish with the scallion greens, and serve with the lemon slices on the side.

To Drink:

An unoaked Chardonnay like Louis Latour Saint-Veran

Poaching salmon in olive oil—simmering it, actually, in an oil-based tapenade—ensures fish that's lusciously tender. You'll want to try this technique with other fish, like tuna or halibut. Flavored with Thai basil, the tapenade is not only used as cooking medium but is served over the fish. I like to accompany this with couscous, but you could also serve it with crusty bread.

OLIVE OIL-POACHED SALMON
with Tomato Tapenade

SERVES 4

1 cup extra-virgin olive oil

1 tablespoon fermented black beans

1 cup pitted Niçoise olives or other oil-cured black olives

1 large onion, thinly sliced

One 28-ounce can plum tomatoes, drained, crushed by hand to remove as much juice as possible, and coarsely chopped

Kosher salt and freshly ground black pepper

Four 6- to 8-ounce skinless salmon fillets, any pin bones removed, cut into fingers approximately 5-by-1-by-1 inch

Leaves from 1 bunch Thai basil or regular basil

3 cups baby arugula or leaves from regular basil, washed and dried

3 lemons, juice of 1, zest of another, the third cut into wedges

1 Preheat the oven to 200°F. Put the oil in a flameproof, 9-by-9-inch straight-sided baking dish, preferably with a lid. Add the black beans, olives, and onion and heat over medium heat until the mixture simmers. Continue to simmer until the onion has begun to soften, about 3 minutes. Add the tomatoes, season with salt and pepper, and simmer until the tomatoes have melted, about 8 minutes.

2 Transfer three-quarters of the tapenade mixture to a medium bowl. Season the salmon with salt and pepper. Add the salmon to the pan and top with a handful of the basil. Spoon the remaining tapenade over it so the fish is completely submerged. Cover with the lid or foil and bake the salmon for 8 to 10 minutes for medium. Place a handful of the arugula on individual plates, drizzle with the lemon juice, and season with salt and pepper. Using a slotted spoon, transfer the salmon to the plates atop the arugula, top with the tapenade, garnish with the lemon zest, and serve.

Video tip:

Watch the video to learn all about the flavor umami.

To Drink:

A Blanc de Blanc Champagne, like Charles de Fere Brut Reserve or Gosset Brut Excellence

CHAPTER 4

Meat

When asked if I like meat, I raise my hand. High. There's nothing quite as satisfying as a juicy steak, a sweet pork roast, or a good, slow-cooked shank. But they're just the start. The recipes here take anyone's meat jones for a major ride.

Case in point: Teriyaki Hanger Steak with Garlic Yukon Mashers, a great family dish that transforms the time-tested marinated steak dish by adding potatoes and a ginger-citrus drizzle. Bell Peppers Stuffed with Spicy Pork Fried Rice get their wallop from a stuffing that includes, besides pork, a fried-rice mixture flavored with ginger and garlic. And Pork Chops with Dried Cranberry-Apple Sweet Potato Hash amps up the humble pork chop and sweet potato pairing by adding a tempting foil of dried fruit and tart apples.

Retooling traditional dishes is my pleasure, but that doesn't mean the "new" dish has to be fancy. Caramelized Onion and Beef "Loco-Moco," based on the traditional Hawaiian rib-sticker of hamburger patties and fried eggs, gets a simplified, family-pleasing take. Braised 8-Spice Lamb Shoulder with Couscous is another homey dish that friends adore too. For family or company, serve meat and its fans rejoice.

When my kids smell this dish cooking—the aroma of garlic, ginger, caramelized sugar, and seared steak combined—there's no question that plates will be cleaned. Adults are equally enthusiastic, so this is a family dish par excellence. Garlic lovers particularly rejoice when they taste the mashers, which are made with roasted garlic heads. Need I say more?

TERIYAKI HANGER STEAK
with Garlic Yukon Mashers

SERVES 4

MARINADE

1 cup naturally brewed soy sauce

1 tablespoon minced garlic

1 tablespoon minced ginger

1 bunch scallions, green and white parts separated, thinly sliced

2 tablespoons light or dark brown sugar

Juice and zest of 2 oranges, 1 tablespoon zest reserved for garnish

2 pounds hanger steak, trimmed and cut into 4 equal pieces

6 Yukon Gold potatoes, washed

2 large or 4 small heads garlic

Kosher salt and freshly ground black pepper

1 tablespoon canola oil

1 tablespoon unsalted butter

1½ cups nonfat plain Greek yogurt

To Drink:

A Meritage like Cameron Hughes Lot 171, from California, or Cain Cuvée

1 Make the marinade: In a large bowl, combine the soy sauce, minced garlic, ginger, scallion whites, brown sugar, orange juice and all but the reserved zest and stir. Add the steak, turn to coat, and marinate for at least 6 and up to 12 hours, refrigerated. Remove the meat and transfer the marinade to a small saucepan.

2 Preheat the oven to 350°F. Wrap the potatoes in foil and pierce several times with a fork. Cut the tops off the garlic heads, season with salt and pepper, and wrap individually in foil. Put the garlic in a small baking dish and place the potatoes and garlic in the oven. Bake until soft and tender, 45 minutes to 1 hour. Transfer the potatoes to a medium bowl and the garlic to a plate and set aside.

3 Heat a large cast-iron skillet or ovenproof pan over high heat. Add the oil and swirl to coat the pan. Remove the steak from the marinade and season with salt and pepper on both sides. When the oil is hot, add the steak and sauté until it colors, 2 to 3 minutes per side. Transfer the steak in the skillet to the oven and roast for 8 to 10 minutes for medium-rare (130°F on a meat thermometer inserted into the thickest part of the steak), 10 to 12 minutes for medium (140°F). Transfer the steak to a cutting board, let rest for 10 minutes, and cut into ¼-inch-thick slices.

4 Meanwhile, bring the marinade to a boil over medium heat. Lower the heat and simmer until the marinade is reduced by one-quarter, about 6 minutes. Remove from the heat and whisk in the butter.

5 Squeeze the garlic from the cloves into the bowl with the potatoes and, with a potato masher or 2 large forks, mash everything roughly, skin and all. Add the yogurt and season with salt and pepper. Stir to blend.

6 Divide the potatoes among 4 individual plates. Top with the steak, drizzle with the sauce, garnish with the reserved zest and the scallion greens, and serve.

I love Hawaiian food—from big-eye tuna to loco-moco, a seriously rib-sticking breakfast dish of rice topped with hamburger patties, onions and fried eggs. Here's my simpler, more refined version that works beautifully for lunch or a homey supper. Kids dig right in, and so do adults. You can of course have loco-moco for breakfast—in which case I advise major post-meal surfing.

CARAMELIZED ONION AND BEEF
"Loco-Moco"

SERVES 4

3 tablespoons canola oil

3 large onions, sliced ¼ inch thick

Kosher salt and freshly ground
   black pepper

1½ pounds ground beef

2 bunches scallions, white and
   green parts, sliced ¼ inch thick,
   1 tablespoon greens reserved
   for garnish

1 tablespoon minced garlic

1 tablespoon plus 1 teaspoon
   naturally brewed soy sauce

2 cups fresh beef or chicken stock or
   low-sodium bought

1 tablespoon cornstarch mixed with
   1 tablespoon water

4 large eggs

6 cups 50-50 White and Brown Rice
   (page 13)

1 Heat a large heavy sauté pan or wok over medium-high heat. Add 1 tablespoon oil and swirl to coat the pan. When the oil is hot, add the onions, season with salt and pepper, and cook on one side until caramelized, 4 to 5 minutes. Turn, cook on the second side for about 5 minutes, then set the onions aside. Reserve the pan.

2 Meanwhile, in a medium bowl, combine the beef, all but the reserved scallions, the garlic and 1 tablespoon of the soy sauce and season with pepper. Mix and form gently into 4 patties about ½ inch thick.

3 Heat the pan over medium-high heat, add 1 tablespoon of the oil, and swirl to coat the pan. Season the patties on both sides with salt and pepper, transfer to the pan, and cook, turning once, for about 4 minutes for medium-rare, 5 minutes for well-done. Transfer the patties to a plate to rest for 5 minutes.

4 Return the pan to medium heat, and add the onions. Pour in the stock, bring to a simmer and add the remaining 1 teaspoon soy sauce. Whisk in the cornstarch slurry and simmer until the sauce is slightly thickened, about 1 minute. Taste to adjust the seasoning with salt and pepper, if necessary.

5 Break the eggs into a bowl. Heat a medium nonstick sauté pan over medium heat. Add the remaining 1 tablespoon of oil and when hot, gently slide in the eggs. Cook for about 1 minute, turn, and cook until the whites are set and the yolks are still soft, about 2 minutes. (If you prefer your eggs sunny side up, add the eggs, cover, cook for about 1 minute, uncover, then cook until the whites are set and the yolks are still soft, 2 to 3 minutes.) Season with salt and pepper.

6 Divide the rice among 4 soup plates or serving bowls, top with the burgers and top with the onions. With a nonmetal spatula, separate the eggs, transfer to the onions, garnish with the reserved scallion greens, and serve.

To Drink:
A chilled lager, like Yanjing

Ming's tips:

Most people like their burgers on the rare side, but for this dish, rare or well-done work equally well. For tender burgers, form the patties as lightly as possible. Then, to ensure even cooking, make an indention with your thumb halfway into the center of each.

To avoid contamination from cutlery, crack the eggs against the side of a counter, or against one another. The method for making the eggs—pouring all the eggs from a bowl into the hot pan and, when cooked, separating them with a spatula—is good to know when preparing fried eggs for a crowd.

The first person to stuff a bell pepper was a genius. While flavorful, most peppers taste pretty much the same—it's the stuffing that makes the difference. Here, peppers are filled with a savory mixture of sausage meat plus spicy fried rice, an Asian touch that makes the dish soar. Served on a bed of spinach dressed with lemon juice, these make a perfect family supper.

BELL PEPPERS STUFFED WITH SPICY PORK FRIED RICE

SERVES 4

4 large red bell peppers
5 tablespoons canola oil, plus more
  for coating the peppers
Kosher salt and freshly ground
  black pepper
4 large eggs, beaten
1 pound spicy Italian sausage meat
1 tablespoon minced ginger
1 tablespoon minced garlic
1 jalapeño pepper, minced
2 bunches scallions, white and green
  parts separated, thinly sliced,
  3 tablespoons of the greens
  reserved for garnish
4 cups 50-50 White and Brown Rice,
  cooked and cooled (page 13)
1 tablespoon wheat-free tamari
8 ounces baby spinach leaves
Juice of 1 lemon

1 Preheat the oven to 350°F. Remove the stems from the peppers and cut off the tops. Mince the tops and set aside. Remove the pepper seeds and ribs. Coat the peppers inside and out with oil, season with salt and pepper, and transfer to a baking dish. Bake until the peppers have softened, 10 to 12 minutes.

2 Cover a large dish with paper towels. Season the eggs with salt and pepper. Heat a large sauté pan over high heat. Add 4 tablespoons of the oil and swirl to coat the pan. When the oil is almost smoking, add the eggs and scramble, stirring constantly, about 15 seconds. Transfer the eggs to the paper towels to drain.

3 In the same pan, over medium-high heat, sauté the sausage meat, breaking it up, until cooked through, 6 to 8 minutes. Transfer to a medium plate and set aside.

4 Return the pan to medium-high heat. Add the remaining 1 tablespoon oil and swirl to coat the pan. When the oil is hot, add the ginger, garlic, jalapeño and all but the reserved scallion greens. Season with salt and pepper. Add the rice, tamari, eggs, sausage meat and reserved minced peppers and heat through, stirring, 2 to 3 minutes. Adjust the seasoning if necessary.

5 In a medium bowl, combine the spinach with the lemon juice, season with salt and pepper and toss. Stuff the peppers with the rice mixture. Place on top of beds of spinach, garnish with the scallion greens, and serve.

To Drink:
Yanjing or Sapporo Premium beer

Pork with fruit is a natural combo, and one that appears in many cultures. The Chinese have sweet and sour pork with pineapple, for example, and we Americans enjoy pork with applesauce. For this easy pork-chop dish I've upped the ante by combining dried fruit—cranberries—with fresh, tart apples. I've also added a hash made from nature's most nutritious spud, the sweet potato, so the dish really takes off.

PORK CHOPS
with Dried Cranberry-Apple Sweet Potato Hash

SERVES 4

1 tablespoon paprika
1 teaspoon ground ginger
1 tablespoon sugar
1 tablespoon kosher salt, plus more
  for seasoning
4 large, thick loin or rib pork chops
3 tablespoons canola oil
1 large red onion, cut into
  ½-inch dice
1 tablespoon minced ginger
2 large sweet potatoes, unpeeled,
  squared and cut into
  1-inch pieces
Freshly ground back pepper
1 cup dried cranberries
2 Granny Smith apples, peeled,
  cored, and cut into 1-inch pieces
½ cup dark rum

1 Preheat the oven to 400°F. Make the rub: In a small bowl, combine the paprika, ground ginger, sugar, and 1 tablespoon salt. Blend and rub well into the chops. Set aside in the refrigerator for 4 hours.

2 Heat a large ovenproof sauté pan over medium-high heat. Add 2 tablespoons of the oil and swirl to coat the pan. When the oil is hot, add the chops and cook on both sides until browned, about 1 minute per side. Remove the chops and set aside.

3 Add the remaining 1 tablespoon of oil, and swirl to coat the pan. When the oil is hot, add the onion, minced ginger and sweet potatoes, season with salt and pepper, and sauté, stirring, for 3 minutes. Add the craisins, apples and rum and flambé. Top with the chops and transfer the pan to the oven. Roast until the pork is cooked but still pink in the center, 10 to 12 minutes, or to 135°F on a meat thermometer. Bring to the table in the pan and serve.

Ming's tips:

Don't buy pork chops with a set idea about getting a loin or rib cut. Instead, go by which looks best.

To flambé the rum using a gas flame, avert your face and tilt the pan into gas. Over an electric burner, allow the rum to heat, then ignite it with a long kitchen match or an automatic lighter.

To Drink:

A bright young Pinot Noir or chilled Gamay Beaujolais, like Laboure-Roi Beaujolais-Villages Saint Armand

In an outdoor restaurant in Morocco I had a terrific dish of boned lamb shoulder cooked over coals and served with a mountain of couscous. It inspired this super-spicy version that features couscous made traditionally—steamed over cooking meat. Besides providing subtle flavor, steaming gives couscous a wonderful fluffy texture. I love lamb shoulder. It has luscious pockets of fat that flavor the meat as it braises. This is a perfect dish to serve to food-loving friends.

BRAISED 8-SPICE LAMB SHOULDER
with Couscous

SERVES 4

3 cups regular (not quick-cooking) couscous

2½ pounds trimmed lamb shoulder, cut into 1-inch cubes

Kosher salt

Canola oil for searing the meat

2 large onions, cut into 1-inch pieces

Cloves from 1 head garlic, peeled and smashed

1 pound carrot nubs

1 bunch celery, ribs cut into 1-inch lengths

1 banana, peeled

RUB

1 tablespoon ground coriander

1 tablespoon ground cumin

1 tablespoon freshly ground black pepper

1 tablespoon paprika

1 tablespoon cayenne

1 tablespoon ground ginger

1 tablespoon ground fennel seeds

1 tablespoon ground cinnamon

To Drink:

A Rhone GSM, like JL Colombo Les Abielles Côtes du Rhone Rouge

1 Put the couscous in a large bowl. Add room-temperature water to cover and let stand for 30 minutes. Set aside.

2 Make the rub: In a small bowl, combine the coriander, cumin, pepper, paprika, cayenne, ginger, fennel and cinnamon and blend.

3 Season the lamb with salt and coat with the rub. (You may not need it all. Save any extra for seasoning steak or chicken.)

4 Heat a large stock pot or Dutch oven over high heat. Add 2 tablespoons of the oil and swirl to coat the bottom. When the oil is hot, and working in batches, add the meat and sear on all sides just until colored, about 6 minutes. Wipe out the pot between batches to avoid burning the spices and use additional oil for each batch. Transfer the meat to a large plate.

5 Without wiping out the pot, add the onions, garlic, carrots and celery and season with salt and pepper. Sauté over medium-high heat, stirring, for 2 minutes. Return the meat with its juices to the pot and add enough water to almost cover the meat. Adjust the seasoning if necessary, add the banana and bring to a simmer. Cover and cook for 30 minutes.

6 Meanwhile, line a colander or steamer basket that will fit into the pot with cheesecloth and place the couscous in it. When the meat has cooked for 30 minutes, fit the colander into the top of the pot and cover with foil, crimping it tightly around the pot's edge to avoid steam escaping. Simmer until the meat is tender and the couscous is cooked, 1 to 1¼ hours. If the banana hasn't disintegrated, mash it into the liquid. Transfer the couscous to a large deep platter, top with the lamb, and serve with bowls of broth.

Ming's tip:

If you have a sturdy metal steamer, by all means use it to braise the meat and steam the couscous.

Our Blue Ginger Burger, which has gained some fame in the burger wars, is packed with umami—that savory "fifth taste" present in cheese and mushrooms, among other ingredients. Specifically, the burger contains a Parmesan and shiitake tuile—delicious, but laborious to make. Here's my easy-to-do version that keeps the cheese and mushrooms in the burger and also features a spicy mayo spread. Serve these with your favorite chips.

SHIITAKE AND PARMESAN HAMBURGER

SERVES 4

3 tablespoons canola oil

2 large shallots, minced

1 pound shiitake mushrooms, stemmed and roughly chopped

Kosher salt and freshly ground black pepper

2 pounds ground beef

1 cup shredded Parmesan

4 tablespoons Dijon mustard

3 tablespoons mayonnaise

4 dashes sriracha or other hot sauce like Frank's or Tabasco sauce

4 best-quality hamburger buns

1 head iceberg lettuce, shredded

1 large tomato, cut into ¼-inch slices

1 Heat a large sauté pan over medium-high heat. Add 1 tablespoon of the oil and swirl to coat the pan. When the oil is hot, add the shallots, sweat them for 30 seconds to 1 minute, then add the shiitakes. Season with salt and pepper and sauté, stirring, until the shiitakes are soft, about 4 minutes. Set aside to cool. Reserve the pan.

2 Meanwhile, in a medium bowl, combine the meat with the Parmesan. When the mushroom mixture is cool, add to the meat and mix lightly. Gently form 4 burgers and season with salt and pepper. Heat the pan over medium heat. Add the remaining 2 tablespoons oil and swirl to coat the pan. When the oil is hot, add the burgers and cook for about 4 minutes. Turn the burgers, lower the heat to medium-low, and continue to cook for 5 to 6 minutes for medium-rare.

3 Meanwhile, in a small bowl, combine the mustard, mayonnaise and sriracha. Toast the buns and spread the mustard mixture on both crumb sides. Top the bottom halves with the lettuce and add the burgers. Season the tomato slices with salt and pepper and place on top of the burgers. Top with the remaining bun halves and serve.

Ming's tips:

Remember to form the burgers lightly, compressing them only until the meat coheres. And don't press them with a spatula as they cook, which can force juices into the pan.

If tomatoes aren't in season, omit them rather than using inferior specimens.

Video tip:

Watch the video for my simple technique for mincing a shallot.

To Drink:

Yanjing beer or an Oregon Pinot Noir, like Four Graces

This was inspired by the classic Italian dish veal Marsala. But instead of the usual mushrooms, I use meaty shiitakes, and port in place of the traditional fortified wine. The bigger news is that I sub pork for the veal—blame it on my Chinese ancestry. Besides being cheaper than veal, pork, with its luscious fat, is really terrific in this dish. The panko makes a particularly delicate crust—I recommend it for most breading. This is a great dinner party dish.

PANKO-CRUSTED PORK CUTLETS
with Mushroom Sauce

SERVES 4

2 pounds pork loin, cut into
　4 equal pieces
1 cup whole-wheat flour or
　all-purpose flour
3 large eggs
2 cups panko
¼ cup chopped parsley, plus more
　for garnish
2 lemons, the juice of 1, the zest of 2
Kosher salt and freshly ground
　black pepper
5 tablespoons canola oil
2 large shallots, thinly sliced
1 pound mushrooms, thinly sliced
1 cup ruby port or dry sherry
1½ cups fresh chicken stock or
　low-sodium bought
½ tablespoon cornstarch mixed with
　½ tablespoon cold water

To Drink:

A New World Pinot Noir, like
Veramonte Ritual, from Chile

1 Preheat the oven to 250°F. Put the pork on a large cutting board and cover with a doubled-up sheet of plastic wrap. Using a mallet or heavy small sauté pan, pound the pork to a thickness of ⅓ inch.

2 Put the flour, eggs and panko in separate shallow dishes. Beat the eggs until well combined. Add the ¼ cup parsley and half the lemon zest to the panko and stir to blend.

3 Season the pork lightly on both sides with salt and pepper. Dredge the pork in the flour, dip in the egg, drain the excess, then dredge in the panko. Transfer to a large plate.

4 Heat a large skillet or sauté pan over medium-high heat. Add 2 tablespoons of the oil and swirl to coat the pan. When the oil is hot, and working in 2 batches with 2 more tablespoons oil, add the pork and sauté, turning once, until golden, 2 to 3 minutes per side. As each cutlet is done, transfer it to a plate and keep warm in the oven. Repeat with the remaining pork.

5 Wipe out the pan and heat over high heat. Add the remaining 1 tablespoon oil and swirl to coat the pan. When the oil is hot add the shallots and sauté, without stirring, until soft, about 1 minute. Add the mushrooms and sauté, stirring, until browned, about 3 minutes. Add the port and lemon juice, stir, and simmer until the liquid is reduced by half, about 2 minutes. Add the stock and bring to a simmer. Whisk in 1 teaspoon of the cornstarch slurry and simmer until lightly thickened, about 1 minute. Adjust the seasoning, if necessary.

6 Transfer the mushroom mixture to a rimmed serving platter and top with the cutlets. Garnish with the extra parsley and remaining zest and serve.

Ming's tip:

When cooking a whole pork shoulder, I would brine the meat to keep in the moisture. But as these are smaller cutlets, no bringing is necessary.

Video tip:

Watch the video to learn my simple technique for mincing fresh parsley.

Not every curry is Indian or contains curry powder. Curries are made throughout Southeast Asia, and can include all sorts of spicy ingredients, wet and dry. Case in point, this terrific Thai-influenced red curry that owes its color to chile powder and paprika. Carrots and sweet potatoes add contrast to its heat, as does the coconut milk, and the pork itself. This is very easy to put together for a quick weeknight meal.

RED CURRY BRAISED PORK ON RICE

SERVES 4

3 tablespoons canola oil, plus more if needed

2 pounds pork shoulder, trimmed and cut into 1-inch cubes

Kosher salt and freshly ground black pepper

2 large onions, cut into 1-inch pieces

1 tablespoon minced ginger

2 red or green jalapeño peppers, minced

1 tablespoon chile powder

1 tablespoon paprika

1 pound carrot nubs

2 large sweet potatoes, peeled and cut into 1-inch dice

1 cup unsweetened coconut milk

1 bay leaf

Juice of 1 lime

6 cups 50-50 White and Brown Rice (page 13)

1 Heat a stock pot over medium-high heat. Add 2 tablespoons of the oil and swirl to coat the bottom. When the oil is hot, and working in batches with additional oil if necessary, add the pork, season with salt and pepper, and color on all sides, 4 to 6 minutes. Transfer the pork to a plate.

2 To the same pot, add the remaining 1 tablespoon oil and swirl to coat the bottom. Add the onions, ginger, and jalapeños and sauté over medium-high heat, stirring, until the onions are lightly brown, about 5 minutes. Add the chile powder and paprika and sauté, stirring, for 30 seconds. Add the carrots, sweet potatoes, coconut milk, and bay leaf and add water to cover the vegetables by 1 inch. Adjust the seasoning, if necessary, and return the pork to the pot. If the pork isn't completely covered, add more water. Bring to a simmer, cover, and cook until the pork is tender, about 1½ hours. Remove the bay leaf and add the lime juice, stir, and serve with rice.

Ming's tip:

You can make this dish in a pressure cooker to save time. Follow the instructions up to the final braising and lock the lid in place according to the manufacturer's instructions. When the steam begins to hiss out of the cooker, reduce the heat to low, just enough to maintain a very weak whistle, and cook for 45 minutes.

Video tip:

Watch the video to see me cook this dish in a pressure cooker.

To Drink:

A Riesling, like Weingut Johann Haart Piesporter Treppchen

This began as a squab dish. Then I got the idea to use an equally full-flavored meat, ground lamb, instead. This in turn proposed the sambal-yogurt accompaniment, a delicious Asian-Greek mashup. Apricots sweeten the sautéed lamb, which is served in crisp lettuce cups. In short, this is a terrific medley of contrasting flavors, textures and even temperatures, given the cooling yogurt.

APRICOT LAMB LETTUCE CUPS
with Sambal Yogurt

SERVES 4

½ cup slivered almonds

1 tablespoon sambal or other chile paste

1 cup nonfat plain Greek yogurt

½ cup chopped dried apricots, preferably unsulfured

1 bunch scallions, white and greens parts separated, thinly sliced

1 tablespoon canola oil

1 pound ground lamb

Kosher salt and freshly ground black pepper

1 tablespoon ground coriander

1 tablespoon minced garlic

2 large leeks, white parts, cut into ½-inch dice (see Tip)

1 cup shredded carrots

Palm-size leaves from 1 head iceberg lettuce

1 Heat a small sauté pan over medium-high heat. Add the almonds and toast, stirring for 1 to 2 minutes. Transfer to a plate and set aside.

2 In a medium bowl, combine the sambal, yogurt, apricots and scallion greens. Mix and set aside.

3 Heat a wok or large sauté pan over high heat. Add the oil and swirl to coat the pan. When the oil is hot, add the lamb and sauté, breaking up the meat, until it loses color, 3 to 4 minutes. Add the coriander, and continue to sauté, stirring, until the lamb is cooked through, 3 to 4 minutes. With a slotted spoon, transfer the meat to a plate.

4 Add the garlic, leeks, and scallion whites to the pan, season with salt and pepper, and cook over medium heat, stirring occasionally, until the vegetables are soft but not colored, 4 to 5 minutes. Add the carrots and lamb to the pan. Stir and heat through, about 2 minutes.

5 Transfer the lettuce cups to a platter or plates. Fill the cups with the lamb mixture and garnish with the almonds. Serve with the yogurt dolloped on top or on the side.

Ming's tip:

To dice the leeks easily, remove most of the green parts, leaving a bit attached to the white, and trim the root ends. Slice the leeks vertically, without cutting into the green ends. Turn the leeks, slice, turn and slice again, so each leek has been cut into sixths. Fill a spinner bowl with water. Cut the white parts of the leeks into ½-inch dice, transfer to the water, and swish with your hands to remove any sand. Pour the leeks with the water into the spinner insert, rinse the leeks under running water to remove any transferred grit, and spin the leeks dry.

To Drink:

A Côte du Rhone or GSM blend, like Gran Clos Finca el Puig Priorat, from Spain

CHAPTER 5

Poultry

Everyone loves chicken. It's versatile, affordable and tasty. My challenge is to use it in fresh ways—either by recasting traditional recipes or creating something new.

Old-into-new, I offer Best-Ever Roast Chicken with Gingered Sweet Potatoes, a luscious pairing of the bird with sweets that are roasted with it, and Wok-Stirred Chile 'n' Cashew Chicken, my fiery, cashew-laced take on kung pao chicken and a great family dish. Crispy Wings in Sweet Chile Sauce will become your default wing dish—and for the best, moistest meatloaf ever, I present Chicken-Onion Meatloaf with Sambal-Worcestershire Gravy, made super-flavorful with chicken dark meat.

As for "new," you can't do better than Soy-Sake Roasted Chicken 'n' Eggs, a pairing of braised eggs, a traditional Chinese favorite, and roast chicken legs and thighs. A totally special dish, this delights guests.

I don't neglect other birds. Turkey Scaloppini with Black Bean–Onion Sauce and Spinach makes use of convenient turkey breast for the scaloppini, and is the best reason I know to serve the bird often. Pan-Roasted Duck Breast with Mushroom Fricassee pairs luscious duck breast with shiitakes and oyster mushrooms, a deeply satisfying marriage. It's yet another reason to enjoy poultry, and for all occasions.

One of my fondest Paris memories is of the street-aroma of cooking rotisserie chickens. Your nose often makes eating decisions for you, and I enjoyed *lots* of those chickens there. Normally, we can't make rotisserie chicken at home, but roasting is a wonderful way to duplicate rotisserie savor. And what's better than serving the roasted bird with sweet potatoes that have cooked in its delicious fat? Nothing!

BEST-EVER ROAST CHICKEN
with Gingered Sweet Potatoes

SERVES 6

⅓ cup kosher salt, for brining, plus more to season

⅓ cup sugar

One six- to eight-pound chicken

3 tablespoons extra-virgin olive oil

2 tablespoons minced garlic

2 tablespoons minced fresh thyme

Freshly ground black pepper

1 tablespoon minced ginger

2 tablespoons agave syrup or honey

3 large sweet potatoes, peeled, squared and cut into 1-inch pieces

1 bunch scallions, white and green parts, thinly sliced

1 The day before, brine the chicken: In a large pitcher, combine the ⅓ cup salt and the sugar with 8 cups water and stir to dissolve the sugar and salt. Put the chicken in a bowl or pot large enough to hold it and the brine and pour the brine over the chicken. If the chicken isn't covered, make more brine and add it to the bowl. Refrigerate overnight. Rinse the chicken and pat dry.

2 Preheat the oven to 500°F. Place a roasting pan on the middle oven rack and heat.

3 Rub the chicken inside and out with 2 tablespoons olive oil, the garlic and 1 tablespoon of the thyme. Season with salt and pepper inside and out.

4 In a large bowl, combine the ginger, syrup, sweet potatoes, scallions, the remaining 1 tablespoon thyme, and the remaining 1 tablespoon oil. Mix well and season with salt and pepper.

5 Pull out the oven rack with the pan and add the vegetables, which will sizzle. Top with the chicken, breast side up, and roast for 15 minutes. Lower the oven temperature to 375°F and continue to roast, turning the pan once front to back, and stirring the potatoes halfway through cooking, until the chicken is done, 1¼ hours longer or until the chicken registers an internal temperature of 160°F on a meat thermometer. If the chicken is coloring too quickly, tent it with foil. Remove the tent 10 minutes before the chicken is cooked so the skin crisps.

6 Transfer the chicken to a cutting board to rest for 10 minutes. Transfer the sweet potatoes to a platter. Carve the chicken, place on top of the potatoes, spoon pan juices over the chicken and serve.

To Drink:

An unoaked Chardonnay, like Qupé Bien Nacido "Y" Block, from California

Kung pao chicken, the spicy, peanut-garnished Hunan dish, is a great family fave. I love peanuts, but for this dish, I love cashews more, and you will too. Traditional "kung pao" is usually made with chicken breast; I use skinless thigh meat, which is much more flavorful but has about the same calories as the white meat. This delicious dish is also very easy on the pocketbook.

WOK-STIRRED CHILE 'N' CASHEW CHICKEN

SERVES 4

4 tablespoons canola oil

1 cup salted roasted cashews

1 teaspoon cayenne pepper, or to taste

1 tablespoon honey

2 pounds boneless, skinless chicken thighs, cut into ½-inch pieces

Kosher salt and freshly ground black pepper

2 jalapeño peppers or serrano chiles with seeds, thinly sliced

1 large onion, cut into ½-inch pieces

1 large red bell pepper, cut into ½-inch pieces

¼ cup white wine or fresh chicken stock or low-sodium bought

2 tablespoons vegetarian oyster sauce

4 cups 50-50 White and Brown Rice (page 13)

1 Heat a wok or large sauté pan over high heat. Add 1 tablespoon of the oil and swirl to coat the pan. When the oil is hot, add the cashews and fry, stirring, until darkly colored, about 30 seconds. Transfer the nuts to a medium bowl, add the cayenne and honey, and stir. Set aside.

2 Heat the wok over high heat. Add 2 tablespoons of the oil and swirl to coat the pan. When the oil is hot, add the chicken, season with salt and pepper, and stir-fry until the chicken is cooked through, about 5 minutes. Transfer to a medium bowl and set aside.

3 Heat the wok over high heat. Add the remaining 1 tablespoon oil and swirl to coat the pan. When the oil is hot, add the jalapeños and sauté, stirring, for 30 seconds. Add the onion and bell pepper and stir-fry until softened, about 2 minutes. Return the chicken and all but 1 tablespoon of the cashews to the wok and add the wine. Add the oyster sauce, stir, and adjust the seasoning, if necessary. Transfer to a platter.

4 Divide the rice among 4 rice bowls. Top with some of the stir-fry, reserving the rest for second helpings. Garnish with the reserved cashews and serve.

Ming's tip:

Lightly frying already roasted cashews releases more of their flavor.

Video tip:

Watch the video to learn my simple technique for rolling and chopping bell peppers.

To Drink:

A Riesling, like Domaines Schlumberger Les Princes Abbés

People should enjoy turkey year-long. You don't have to roast a whole one—its breast is a delicious and convenient route to easy turkey dinners. Like chicken breast, though, it can be dry. That's avoided in this delicious recipe by cutting the breast into scaloppini, breading them with tarragon-flavored panko, and then sautéing them until golden—a great way to add flavor as well as sealing in juices. The black bean–onion sauce is a great accompaniment, and the spinach "side" adds its own great taste.

TURKEY SCALOPPINI
with Black Bean–Onion Sauce and Spinach

SERVES 4

1 cup whole-wheat flour or all-purpose flour

3 large eggs

2 cups panko

2 tablespoons minced fresh tarragon

One 3- to 4-pound boneless, skinless turkey breast

Kosher salt and freshly ground black pepper

5 tablespoons canola oil

1 tablespoon extra-virgin olive oil

1 bag (9 to 10 ounces) baby spinach leaves, stemmed, washed and spun dry

Zest and juice of 2 lemons, 2 teaspoons zest reserved for garnish

1 large onion, minced

1 tablespoon minced fermented black beans

2 cups fresh chicken stock or low-sodium bought

2 tablespoons unsalted butter

To Drink:

A chilled Gamay, like Louis Latour Beaujolais Villages

1 Preheat the oven to 250°F.

2 Put the flour, eggs and panko in separate shallow dishes. Add the tarragon to the panko and stir to blend.

3 Remove the tenderloin from the turkey breast (reserve it for another use) and cut the meat on the extreme bias into 1-inch-thick cutlets. Place the cutlets on a cutting board, cover with plastic wrap, and using a mallet or small sauté pan, pound the cutlets until $1/3$ inch thick. Season the turkey on both sides with salt and pepper. Dredge the turkey in the flour, dip in the egg, drain the excess, then dredge in the panko. Transfer to a large plate.

4 Heat a large skillet over medium-high heat. Add 2 tablespoons of the canola oil and swirl to coat the pan. When the oil is hot, add half the turkey scaloppini and sear until brown and cooked through, turning once, about 3 minutes per side. Repeat with 2 more tablespoons oil and the remaining scaloppini. Transfer the turkey to a baking sheet and place in the oven to keep warm.

5 Wipe out the pan and return it to high heat. Add the olive oil and swirl to coat the pan. When the oil is hot, add the spinach and lemon zest and sauté, stirring, for 30 seconds. Season with salt and pepper and sauté, stirring, until the spinach has wilted, about 1 minute. Transfer to a medium bowl.

6 Wipe out the pan and heat over high heat. Add the remaining 1 tablespoon canola oil and swirl to coat the pan. When the oil is hot, add the onion and black beans and sauté, stirring, until the onion is lightly colored, about 2 minutes. Season with salt and pepper. Add the lemon juice and stock, bring to a simmer, and cook until the liquid is reduced by half, about 5 minutes. Whisk in the butter.

7 Transfer the spinach to a platter and top with the turkey. Spoon the pan sauce around, garnish with the reserved lemon zest and serve.

Video tip:

Watch the video to see me break down and pound the turkey breast.·

After years of operation, my mom sold our family restaurant, Mandarin Kitchen, to a Korean couple. The new owners put crispy chicken wings on the menu, which they served with a sweet-spicy, garlicky sauce. I ate a lot of that fabulous dish and begged for the sauce recipe, but I could never get it. When I became a chef, one of my priorities was to reproduce the dish—and here it is, a Blue Ginger favorite. The wings are fantastic for parties and other gatherings. Just make more than you think you'll need, as they disappear fast.

CRISPY WINGS IN SWEET CHILE SAUCE

SERVES 4

3 tablespoons canola oil, plus more for frying

2 red onions, roughly chopped

1 tablespoon minced garlic

2 red or green jalapeño peppers, minced

Kosher salt and freshly ground black pepper

2 red bell peppers, seeded and roughly chopped

1 cup rice vinegar

¼ cup agave syrup or honey

3 pounds chicken wings, drummette and wing ends separated, washed and patted dry

2 tablespoons toasted sesame seeds

1 Heat a medium sauté pan over medium-high heat. Add 1 tablespoon of the oil and swirl to coat the pan. When the pan is hot, add the onions and garlic and sauté, stirring, for 1 minute. Add the jalapeños, season with salt and black pepper, and sauté until soft, about 8 minutes. Add the bell peppers and sauté, stirring, until softened, about 2 minutes. Add the vinegar, stir, and sauté until the liquid is reduced by half, about 5 minutes. Transfer the mixture to a blender and purée, drizzling in the syrup and the remaining 2 tablespoons oil. Season with salt and pepper and continue to purée until the mixture is very smooth. Set aside.

2 Fill a large stock pot halfway with oil. Heat over high heat to 375°F to 400°F on a deep-frying thermometer. Cover a platter with paper towels.

3 Season the wings with salt and pepper. Working in batches, if necessary, add the wings to the oil gradually, and fry until the wings are crisp and golden, 20 to 25 minutes. Transfer to the paper towels to drain, then to a large serving bowl. Add half the sesame seeds and some of the sauce to coat the wings lightly. Garnish with the remaining sesame seeds and serve with the remaining sauce on the side.

To Drink:

Chilled beer, like Sam Adams lager, or Harpoon India Pale Ale

Everyone loves meatloaf—when it's done right. This meatloaf recipe features dark chicken meat, which not only delivers great taste but is better for you than the usual beef. The gravy is flavored with Worcestershire, an underused condiment that's a tart foil for the sambal. I often make this dish just for the leftovers—a sandwich of the sliced loaf on toasted bread with crisp lettuce and hot Dijon mustard will make you very, very happy.

CHICKEN-ONION MEATLOAF
with Sambal-Worcestershire Gravy

SERVES 4

1 tablespoon plus 1 teaspoon canola oil, plus more for oiling the pan

3 large onions, diced

Kosher salt and freshly ground black pepper

2 tablespoons minced garlic

2 pounds ground dark chicken meat

1 cup cooked brown or white rice

½ cup chopped parsley, plus about 12 leaves for garnish

2 cups diced celery

1 tablespoon sambal or other chile seasoning

¼ cup organic Worcestershire sauce

2 cups fresh chicken stock or low-sodium bought

1 tablespoon cornstarch mixed with 1 tablespoon water

1 Preheat the oven to 350°F. Oil a 9-by-5-inch loaf pan.

2 Heat a large sauté pan over medium-high heat. Add 1 tablespoon oil and swirl to coat the pan. When the oil is hot, add the onions, season with salt and pepper, add the garlic and sauté, stirring, until caramelized, about 10 minutes. Transfer two-thirds of the mixture to a large bowl and let cool.

3 Add the chicken, rice and parsley, blend and season with salt and pepper. Test the seasoning by sautéing 1 tablespoon of the mixture in a little hot oil or in a microwave for 20 seconds on high power. Adjust the seasoning with salt and pepper, if necessary.

4 Transfer the mixture to the pan without packing it tightly and pat the top smooth. Bake until cooked through, about 45 minutes, or until a knife inserted in the middle of the loaf comes out clean. Let stand for 10 minutes, then unmold, and slice. Transfer the slices to a platter or individual plates.

5 Meanwhile, heat the pan with the remaining onion mixture over medium-high heat. Add the 1 teaspoon of oil and swirl to coat the pan. Add the celery, season with salt and pepper and sauté, stirring, until soft, about 3 minutes. Add the sambal, Worcestershire sauce, stock and meat drippings, bring to a simmer, and cook to reduce by one-quarter, 3 to 4 minutes. Whisk in three-quarters of the cornstarch slurry in a thin stream, season with salt and pepper, and simmer until lightly thickened, about 3 minutes. Spoon the sauce over the meatloaf, garnish with the parsley leaves, and serve.

To Drink:

A spicy California Zinfandel, like Ridge East Bench

Ming's tip:

The recipe directs you to test the loaf mixture for seasoning by cooking a bit of it. This may seem fussy, but it's really necessary to ensure best flavor.

The first time I had pineapple fried rice was in Hawaii. It was made by restaurateur and chef Sam Choy, and contained Spam. I had my doubts about that popular Hawaiian ingredient, but the dish was delicious, and is the inspiration for this version, which features chicken sausage meat rather than Spam. The spicy chicken is a perfect match for the fresh pineapple, and the whole dish a satisfying meal-in-one.

CHICKEN SAUSAGE FRIED RICE
with Pineapple

SERVES 4

2 tablespoons canola oil

1½ pounds chicken sausage meat, preferably Italian

1 English cucumber, very thinly sliced (see Tip, page 67)

Juice and zest of 1 lemon

1 teaspoon toasted sesame oil

Kosher salt and freshly ground black pepper

5 cloves garlic, sliced as thin as possible

1 tablespoon minced ginger

1 bunch scallions, white and green parts, thinly sliced, 2 tablespoons of the greens reserved for garnish

1 tablespoon sambal

½ pineapple, peeled, cored and diced

1 large red bell pepper, diced

6 cups 50-50 White and Brown Rice, cooked and cooled (page 13)

1 tablespoon wheat-free tamari

1 Heat a wok over high heat. Add 1 tablespoon of the canola oil and swirl to coat the pan. When the oil is hot, add the sausage and sauté, breaking up the meat, until cooked through, 6 to 8 minutes. Transfer to a plate.

2 Heat the wok over high heat. Add the remaining 1 tablespoon canola oil and swirl to coat the pan. When the oil is hot, add the garlic, ginger, scallions and sambal and sauté, stirring, until fragrant, 30 seconds. Add the pineapple and bell pepper and sauté until the rawness is cooked out, about 1 minute. Add the rice and tamari, season with pepper, and heat through, stirring, for 1 minute. Return the sausage to the pan and heat through, stirring occasionally. Taste to adjust the seasoning with salt and pepper, if necessary.

3 In a medium bowl, combine the cucumber, lemon juice and zest, and sesame oil. Season with salt and black pepper and set aside.

4 Transfer the rice to a large serving bowl. Top with the cucumber mixture, garnish with the scallion greens, and serve.

To Drink:

A Pinot Blanc, like Trimbach

Duck breast is underused by most American cooks. That's a shame, as it's easily prepared—you cook it just like steak—and wonderfully tasty. You also get the bonus of its deliciously crisp skin. Here, the sautéed breasts are paired with a fricassee made from potatoes that are cooked in the duck fat plus oyster and shiitake mushrooms. This is great eating, and pleases diners of every stripe.

PAN-ROASTED DUCK BREAST
with Mushroom Fricassee

SERVES 4

4 duck breasts (about 10 ounces each), preferably Pekin, tenderloin, any sinew and excess fat removed

Kosher salt and freshly ground black pepper

2 large Yukon Gold potatoes, peeled and cut into ½-inch dice

2 shallots, minced

1 tablespoon minced garlic

¾ pound shiitake mushrooms, stems removed, cut into ¼-inch slices

¼ cup dry red wine

¾ pound oyster mushrooms, stems trimmed, large ones torn into 4 pieces, smaller ones torn in half

1 bunch chives, cut into ⅓-inch slices, 1 tablespoon reserved for garnish

1 Score the skin side of the duck breasts in a crosshatch pattern, slicing only halfway through the fat layer.

2 Heat a large heavy sauté pan or cast-iron skillet over medium heat. Season the breasts with salt and pepper, turn the heat to low, and cook, skin side down, until brown and crisp, 20 to 25 minutes. Transfer to a cutting board skin side up, and set aside. Pour off all but 2 tablespoons of the fat into a heatproof bowl and reserve.

3 Return the pan to medium-high heat. When the fat is hot, add the potatoes and season with salt and pepper. Cook the potatoes without stirring until browned, 3 to 4 minutes. Turn over and brown the other side. Continue to turn and cook the potatoes until at least 3 sides are browned and the potatoes are cooked through, another 6 to 7 minutes. Transfer to a plate lined with paper towels and set aside.

4 Put 2 tablespoons of the reserved fat in the pan and swirl to coat. When the fat is hot, add the shallots and garlic, season with salt and pepper and sauté, stirring, for 1 minute. Add the shiitakes and sauté, stirring, until softened, 1 to 2 minutes. Add the wine and deglaze the pan. Add the oyster mushrooms, season with salt and pepper and sauté, stirring, until golden and cooked through, about 2 minutes. Taste to adjust the seasoning. Return the potatoes to the pan and add all but the reserved chives. Stir, adjust the seasoning, if necessary, and transfer to a platter.

5 Wipe out the pan and heat over medium-high heat. Add 1 tablespoon fat and swirl to coat the pan. When the fat is hot, add the breasts meat side down and cook until medium-rare, 1 to 2 minutes. Flip over and cook to re-crisp the skin sides, 1 to 2 minutes. Transfer to a cutting board, slice and place on top of the potatoes. Garnish with the reserved chives and serve.

To Drink:

A French or Oregon Pinot Noir, like Argyle Winery's

Ming's tip:

I like to serve food on hot plates. To warm them easily, run under hot water for 30 seconds then dry them, or heat them in the microwave for 1 minute.

I'm a major fan of leeks, a vegetable I first discovered in France. Leeks are similar to scallions, but have a delightfully sweet edge. They're paired here with dark-meat chicken, carrots, and a homey Yukon Gold mash made with luscious but low-cal Greek yogurt. You can see that this is a delicious, completely satisfying dish that works for weekend family dinners and company alike.

BRAISED CHICKEN AND LEEKS
on Country Mash

SERVES 4 TO 6

5 large Yukon Gold potatoes, washed and dried

2 pounds boneless, skinless chicken thighs, cut into 1-inch pieces

Kosher salt and freshly ground black pepper

4 tablespoons canola oil

3 large leeks, white parts halved, cut into strips, washed and dried (see Tip, page 114)

1 pound carrot nubs

1 cup white wine

2 heaping tablespoons fresh tarragon leaves, roughly chopped, plus additional leaves for garnish

2 tablespoons naturally brewed soy sauce

2 cups fresh chicken stock or low-sodium bought, or water, plus more if needed

1 tablespoon cornstarch mixed with 1 tablespoon water

½ bunch scallions, white and green parts, thinly sliced

2 cups nonfat plain Greek yogurt

1 Preheat the oven to 350°F. Wrap the potatoes in foil, pierce several times with a fork and bake until soft, about 45 minutes.

2 Meanwhile, line a large plate with paper towels. Season the chicken with salt and pepper. Heat a large stock pot or Dutch oven over medium-high heat. Add 2 tablespoons of the oil and swirl to coat the pan. When the oil is hot, add the chicken and brown on all sides, 6 to 8 minutes. Transfer the chicken to the paper towels and set aside.

3 In the same pan, over medium-high heat, and the remaining 2 tablespoons oil and swirl to coat the pan. When the oil is hot, add the leeks and sauté, stirring, until caramelized, 6 to 8 minutes. Add the carrots, stir, and season with salt and pepper. Add the wine, stir, and simmer until the liquid is reduced by one quarter, about 1 minute. Return the chicken to the pan and add the tarragon, soy sauce, and stock. Bring to a simmer and adjust the seasoning with salt and pepper. Reduce the heat, cover, and simmer until the chicken is cooked through, about 25 minutes. Turn the heat to high, whisk in the cornstarch slurry, and cook until thickened, about 30 seconds.

4 Transfer the potatoes to a large bowl and mash roughly with a masher or wooden spoon. Add the scallions and mix well. Add ½ cup of the braising liquid and the yogurt, mix and season with salt and pepper.

5 Strike the reserved tarragon leaves with the heel of your hand to release their fragrance. Transfer the mash to serving bowls, top with the chicken, garnish with the tarragon leaves, and serve.

To Drink:

A crisp French Chardonnay, like a Chablis from Simonnet Febvre

I'm known for my East-West cooking. This dish, however, draws on two Asian cuisines, Japanese and Chinese. The braising liquid contains soy and sake—the Japanese part—and the eggs, which are cracked and cooked in the liquid, are Chinese-inspired. Served with roasted chicken and a tasty slaw, the eggs are wonderfully flavored and beautiful too—once shelled, they show a mosaic pattern made by the soy. As a kid, I enjoyed similar eggs for Easter while my friends ate the candy kind. Nobody envied my eggs, but once you taste their descendents in this terrific dish, you'll understand why I loved Easter.

SOY-SAKE ROASTED CHICKEN 'N' EGGS

SERVES 6

2 cups naturally brewed soy sauce

2 cups sake, preferably Ty Ku Silver

½ cup dark brown sugar

1 tablespoon minced garlic

1 tablespoon minced ginger

6 chicken legs

6 chicken thighs

12 large eggs

2 bunches scallions, white and green parts, cut into ½-inch lengths

One 10-ounce bag shredded carrots

1 small head red cabbage, thinly sliced

Juice and zest of 2 lemons, 1 teaspoon zest reserved for garnish

Freshly ground black pepper

6 cups 50-50 White and Brown Rice (page 13)

1 In a medium bowl, combine the soy sauce, sake, brown sugar, garlic and ginger and stir to combine. Reserve ½ cup of the marinade and set aside. Put the chicken in a large bowl and pour the marinade over it. Turn the chicken to coat it evenly with the marinade, cover and refrigerate for 1 hour.

2 Fill a large bowl with ice and add water. Bring a stock pot half full of water to a boil. Add the eggs, cook for 3½ minutes, and transfer to the bowl. When the eggs are cold, remove and crack the shells gently. Set aside. Dry the pot.

3 Preheat the oven to 400°F and place a baking sheet large enough to hold all the chicken on the middle rack. Drain the chicken, reserve the marinade and transfer the chicken to the baking sheet—the chicken will sizzle. Roast until cooked through, turning the chicken once, about 35 minutes. Glaze with the ½ cup reserved marinade after 10 minutes, after the chicken is turned, and 5 minutes before it's cooked through.

4 In the meantime, add the remaining marinade to the pot and bring to a boil over medium heat. Return the eggs to the pot, add the scallions and carrots, cover and simmer over low heat for 30 minutes. Using a slotted spoon, transfer the eggs to a medium bowl.

5 In a large bowl, combine the cabbage, lemon juice and all but the reserved zest, the cooked carrots and scallions, and toss. Let sit for 10 minutes.

6 Peel the eggs. Place a mound of the cabbage mixture in individual serving bowls. Top each with the chicken leg and thigh and 2 of the eggs. Garnish with the lemon zest and serve with bowls of the rice.

To Drink:

A chilled sake, like Ty Ku Silver

Say Japanese food and most people think sushi. But Japanese cooking is extremely diverse, and shares a number of dishes with other Asian cuisines. Curry is one common dish, as I discovered when I first went to a curry restaurant in Osaka. Japanese curries, which contain pork or chicken, are milder than the Indian kind and are served with rice. This Japanese curry features chicken served with rice and potatoes, which sounds like overkill, but is just right. An awesome cold-weather meal, this is also welcomed when the temperature has climbed.

JAPANESE CHICKEN CURRY
with Potatoes and Rice

SERVES 4

2 tablespoons canola oil

2 large onions, cut into ½-inch dice

2 tablespoons minced ginger

3 tablespoons curry powder, preferably Madras

Kosher salt and freshly ground black pepper

2 pounds boneless, skinless chicken thighs, cut into 1-inch pieces

1 quart fresh chicken stock or low-sodium bought, or water

½ bunch celery, cut into 1-inch pieces

2 large Yukon Gold potatoes, squared and cut into 1-inch cubes

¼ cup roughly chopped flat-leaf parsley, half reserved for garnish

2 tablespoons cornstarch mixed with 2 tablespoons cold water

6 cups 50-50 White and Brown Rice (page 13)

1 Heat a stock pot over medium-high heat. Add the oil and swirl to coat the bottom of the pot. When the oil is hot, add the onions and sweat until soft and lightly colored, 3 to 4 minutes. Add the ginger and curry powder and sauté, stirring occasionally, until aromatic, about 1 minute. Season with salt and pepper.

2 Add the chicken, season with salt and pepper, and add stock just to cover. Add the celery, potatoes, and half the parsley and bring to a simmer. Taste to adjust the seasoning, if necessary. Set a cover ajar on the pot, lower the heat to medium-low, and cook until the chicken is tender, about 45 minutes.

3 Turn the heat to high, whisk in the cornstarch slurry, and cook until the liquid is thickened, about 1 minute.

4 Divide the rice among plates. Top with the chicken, garnish with the reserved parsley, and serve.

Video tips:

Watch the video to learn my simple technique for squaring and dicing potatoes, as well as how to prepare and add the cornstarch slurry and the importance of doing so.

To Drink:

A lager or super clean-tasting Japanese beer, like Sapporo

Everyone loves chicken pad Thai, Thailand's deliciously spicy noodle dish. The noodles used are rice sticks, which, besides being delightfully chewy, are gluten-free (for those allergic to it) and "cooked" simply by soaking. My version is easier to make than many others—I've eliminated the traditional tamarind, which is hard to find and fussy to prepare—but nothing is lost in the flavor department, I promise. I include the traditional scrambled eggs, but you can omit them, if you like. You'll still have a wonderfully satisfying dish.

LEMONGRASS CHICKEN PAD THAI

SERVES 4 TO 6

8 ounces rice sticks

1 pound boneless, skinless chicken thighs, cut into strips ⅓ inch wide

Kosher salt and freshly ground black pepper

3 tablespoons plus 1 teaspoon canola oil

4 lemongrass stalks, white parts only, minced (see Tip, page 166)

1 large red onion, thinly sliced

1 jalapeño pepper, cut into thin rings

3 large eggs, lightly beaten

1 large red bell pepper, seeded and cut into ¼-inch slices (see Tip)

2 tablespoons fish sauce

Juice and zest of 2 lemons

1 Place the noodles in a medium bowl and fill it with hot water to cover. Soak until pliable but not completely soft, 10 to 15 minutes. Drain and set aside.

2 Season the chicken with salt and black pepper. Heat a wok over medium-high heat. Add 2 tablespoons of the oil and swirl to coat the pan. When the oil is hot, add the chicken and stir-fry until brown and cooked through, about 3 minutes. Set aside.

3 Return the wok to medium-high heat. Add the remaining 1 tablespoon oil and swirl to coat. When the oil is hot, add the lemongrass, onion and jalapeño. Stir-fry until the onion is soft, about 1 minute. Push the mixture to one side of the wok, drizzle in the 1 teaspoon oil, and add the eggs. Stir-fry, breaking up the eggs, until the eggs are cooked through, about 30 seconds. When the eggs are set, stir to incorporate the onion mixture.

4 Return the chicken to the pan, add the bell peppers, and stir. Add the fish sauce, lemon juice and zest, and noodles. Stir and cook until heated through, about 2 minutes. Adjust the seasoning with salt and pepper if necessary and transfer to a serving platter or plates, and serve.

Ming's tips:

To slice the red pepper easily, first cut away both ends. Cut downward into the pepper on one long side and "peel" away its flesh by rolling the pepper while you cut. You'll have separated the useable part of the pepper from its core and seeds. Halve the useable part, stack the halves, and slice lengthwise.

The noodle soaking method here, which uses hot water, is fairly quick. But, if you have more time, soak them in room-temperature water for about 2 hours. Whichever method you choose, you're aiming for noodles that are soft but not mushy, as the noodles will continue to cook when heated through before serving.

To Drink:

A Riesling, like S.A. Prum, from Germany

CHAPTER 6

Vegetables, Rice and Noodles

In many cultures, especially those of Asia, grain and vegetable dishes rule. And rightfully so. Alone or combined, they can yield as much flavor, textural interest, and satisfaction as meat dishes. They're also quick to make and usually lighter on the stomach and pocketbook than their meat cousins. When devising them, all you need is some imagination.

To spur inspiration, I often think wok. Three-Mushroom and Jicama Chow Mein, an exciting textural meld, and Wok-Stirred Zucchini and Onions with Black Garlic, which puts deeply flavorful black garlic center stage, are wok-made in minutes. Another wok dish, Crazy Noodle Stir-Fry, is made with chewy rice noodles and seitan, a versatile, wheat-based product I endorse for its great texture and healthfulness. Tofu is another great-for-you ingredient that, in its smoked version, shines in Singapore Curry Tofu Noodles and in Crispy Tofu with Peanut-Garlic Glaze, where it gets a hot-garlicky drizzle—totally delicious!

Couscous and vegetables are traditionally matched. I celebrate that pairing in Veggie Ragout with Couscous and Harissa Sauce, a deeply flavorful meld of eggplant, sweet potatoes, and zucchini, among other ingredients. And rice lovers, which is most of us, will call Eight Treasure Fried Rice and Hunan Glazed Eggplant with Rice their new best friends. Grains and vegetables open dining doors.

This began as a chicken-noodle stir-fry. Then I said to myself, Self, why not make this with tempeh or seitan instead of the poultry? Those wheat- and soy bean-based products have the look and texture of meat and, I soon found, work beautifully in this crazy-fiery dish, as does smoked tofu, another no-meat option. This isn't just for vegetarians; with its satisfying noodles and Thai-inspired flavors, it delights everyone.

CRAZY NOODLE STIR-FRY

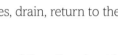

SERVES 4

8 ounces rice sticks

3 tablespoons canola oil

1 large onion, minced

1 tablespoon minced garlic

1 tablespoon minced ginger

Kosher salt and freshly ground
  black pepper

1 tablespoon sambal or hot sauce

3 large eggs, beaten

 pound tempeh, crumbled, or seitan,
  pulsed in a food processor to the
  texture of ground meat

Juice of 2 limes

2 tablespoons naturally brewed
  soy sauce

1 red bell pepper, cut into -inch slices
  (see Tip, page 138)

 cup cilantro leaves, half reserved for
  garnish

1 Put the noodles in a large bowl and fill it with hot water to cover. When the noodles have softened, after about 15 minutes, drain, return to the bowl and set aside.

2 Heat a wok over high heat. Add 2 tablespoons of the oil and swirl to coat the wok. When the oil is hot, add the onion, garlic and ginger and stir-fry until softened, about 2 minutes. Season with salt and pepper.

3 Combine the sambal with the eggs and stir to blend. Add the remaining 1 tablespoon oil to the wok, add the egg mixture, and stir vigorously until the eggs are just cooked through, about 1 minute. Add the tempeh, lime juice and soy sauce and stir-fry for 1 minute. Add the noodles, bell pepper and stir-fry until heated through, 1 to 2 minutes. Taste to adjust the seasoning. Add all but the reserved cilantro and toss. Transfer to individual serving plates, garnish with the remaining cilantro, and serve.

Ming's tips:

For palatability and safety, be sure to heat the seitan, if using, thoroughly in the final step.

I've also had good luck using imitation chicken, a vegetable-based product, in this. Brands I've used are Gardein™ Chic'n Strips and Morningstar Farms™ Meal Starter Chick'n Strips.

Video tip:

Watch the video to see a tutorial on imitation meats.

To Drink:

Ginger ale or iced green tea, sweetened with ginger syrup (page 184), and flavored with lime juice to taste

The day I discovered black garlic I was overjoyed. Made from regular garlic that's fermented and dried, it tastes like a cross between roasted garlic and Chinese black beans. It would be difficult to find a more umami-rich ingredient—I use black garlic often in stir-frys and stews, where it kicks dishes into the stratosphere. Here, it does its thing for a simple zucchini stir-fry that's brightened with fresh mint. The dish turns out to be a major wow.

ZUCCHINI-ONION STIR-FRY
with Black Garlic

SERVES 4

1 tablespoon canola oil

2 large onions, cut into ½-inch dice

Kosher salt and freshly ground black pepper

6 cloves black garlic (see Tip), roughly chopped

1 tablespoon minced ginger

3 large zucchini, roll-cut into 1-inch pieces (see Tip)

1 tablespoon naturally brewed soy sauce

2 cups fresh vegetable stock or low-sodium bought

1 tablespoon cornstarch mixed with 1 tablespoon water

¼ cup mint leaves, torn

6 to 8 cups 50-50 White and Brown Rice (page 13)

1 Heat a wok over high heat. Add the oil and swirl to coat the pan. When the oil is hot, add the onions and stir-fry until soft, about 1 minute. Season with salt and pepper. Add the black garlic and ginger and stir-fry for 1 minute.

2 Add the zucchini, season with salt and stir-fry for 2 minutes, then add the soy sauce and stock. Simmer until the liquid is reduced by one-quarter, 3 to 4 minutes. Whisk in half the cornstarch slurry and simmer until the mixture is glazed and lightly thickened, about 1 minute. Adjust the seasoning with salt and pepper, if necessary. Add the mint, toss, and serve with the rice.

Ming's tips:

Black garlic is available in heads or cloves, which come in airless bags. If you can't get black garlic, use 2 cloves garlic minced with 1 tablespoon fermented black beans.

To roll-cut the zucchini and other vegetables, first slice away stem ends on an angle. Roll the vegetable about a quarter turn away from you and slice again at the same angle about 1 inch farther down or the length your recipe suggests. Continue rolling and slicing until the vegetable has been entirely cut.

To Drink:

A Chardonnay, like Kermit Lynch Eric Chevalier, from the Loire Valley in France

This dish was inspired by the Singaporean hawker-style carrot cake *chai tow kway* and by my maternal grandfather's wonderful daikon pancakes, which also originated in Singapore. My version includes both vegetables for great texture and is characteristically fiery. You can serve these as an appetizer, but they're also good as a main dish with a salad.

SINGAPOREAN CARROT-DAIKON
Pancakes with Chile Sauce

SERVES 4

3 tablespoons canola oil, or more
    if needed
1 tablespoon minced garlic
1 bunch scallions, white and green
    parts, 1 tablespoon of the greens
    reserved for garnish
Kosher salt and freshly ground
    black pepper
1 large daikon, peeled and
    grated
1 large carrot, peeled and
    grated
1 cup rice flour
5 large eggs, beaten
2 heaping teaspoons sambal
3 tablespoons ketjap manis
Juice of 1 lime

1 Heat a large heavy sauté pan or cast-iron skillet over medium-high heat. Add 1 tablespoon of the oil and swirl to coat the pan. When the oil is hot, add the garlic and all but the reserved scallions and sauté, stirring, until fragrant, about 30 seconds. Season with salt and pepper. Add the daikon and carrot and sauté, stirring, until softened, about 2 minutes. Season with salt and transfer to a medium bowl to cool. Wipe out the pan.

2 Add the rice flour to a large bowl and whisk in the eggs to make a batter. Add 1 heaping teaspoon of the sambal and 1 tablespoon of the ketjap manis and whisk to blend. Add the cooled mixture and blend.

3 Line a large plate or platter with paper towels. Heat the pan over medium-high heat. Add the remaining 2 tablespoons oil and swirl to coat the pan. When the oil is hot, ladle enough of the batter into the pan to make 4 pancakes about 2 inches in diameter. Use the bottom of the ladle or spatula to flatten the pancakes to size. Cook until the bottoms have browned, 1 to 2 minutes. Using a large spatula, flip the pancakes and brown the second side, 2 minutes, and transfer to the paper towels to drain. Repeat with the remaining batter, adding more oil if needed.

4 In a small bowl, combine the lime juice, the remaining 1 heaping teaspoon sambal and the remaining 2 tablespoons ketjap manis.

5 Transfer the pancakes to a large serving plate, drizzle with the sambal mixture, garnish with the reserved scallion greens and serve immediately.

To Drink:

A chilled Singapore beer, like Tiger, or Tsing Tao, from China

Ming's tip:

You can make the vegetables and batter ahead of time. Keep covered with plastic wrap in the refrigerator for up to 24 hours, and cook the pancakes when your guests show up.

Years ago I had the best couscous of my life at Le Zerda Cafe in Paris. It was steamed over broth, which gave it great flavor and a light, fluffy texture. I've adopted this method for this great dish, which features a savory ragout of eggplant, sweet potatoes, zucchini and bell peppers. Diners add dollops of harissa mixed with yogurt to their servings, just the right hot-cooling finale. This is another great dinner party dish.

VEGGIE RAGOUT
with Couscous and Harissa Sauce

SERVES 4

10 ounces regular (not quick-cooking) fine whole-wheat couscous

Kosher salt

2 tablespoons extra-virgin olive oil

1 large red onion, cut into ½-inch dice

1 tablespoon minced garlic

1 tablespoon minced ginger

1 tablespoon minced fermented black beans

Freshly ground black pepper

1 large eggplant, diced

2 medium sweet potatoes, peeled and diced

2 large zucchini, cut into ½-inch dice

2 large red bell peppers, diced

1 to 2 tablespoons naturally brewed soy sauce, to taste

One 28-ounce can diced plum tomatoes

1 quart fresh vegetable stock or low-sodium bought

1 tablespoon harissa

1 cup nonfat plain Greek yogurt

1 Put the couscous in a large bowl. Cover with room-temperature water and allow the couscous to soak for 1 hour. Add a pinch of salt and rub it into the couscous, breaking up any lumps.

2 Meanwhile, heat a stock pot or heavy soup pot over medium-high heat. Add the oil and swirl to coat the bottom. When the oil is hot, add the onion, garlic, ginger and black beans and season with salt and pepper. Sauté, stirring, until softened, 2 to 3 minutes. Add the eggplant and sweet potatoes, season with salt and pepper and sauté, stirring, until softened, about 4 minutes. Add the zucchini and sauté, stirring, until tender, about 2 minutes. Season with salt and pepper. Add the bell peppers, soy sauce to taste, tomatoes and stir. Add the stock, taste to adjust the seasoning with salt and pepper, if necessary, and bring to a simmer.

3 Line a colander or steamer basket that will fit into the pot with cheesecloth and place the couscous in it. Fit the colander into the top of the pot and cover with foil, crimping it tightly around the pot's edge to avoid steam escaping. Simmer until the ragout and the couscous are cooked, about 45 minutes.

4 Meanwhile, in a small serving bowl, combine the harissa and yogurt. Season with salt. Mound the couscous in the center of individual plates. Surround with the ragout, and spoon additional liquid from the ragout around it. Dollop the yogurt mixture on top and serve with the remaining mixture on the side.

To Drink:

A Chenin Blanc, like Mulderbosch

This dish is dedicated to my grandfather Yeh Yeh, who came from Hunan, where spicy dishes rule. He made his own sambal with chiles he grew in his Dayton, Ohio garden. As a kid I would try to outdo him in the how-hot-can-you-take-it eating department—let's just say that I did my very best. This great eggplant medley touches all the Hunanese flavor bases—it's savory, sweet and tart as well as spicy, and satisfies non-meat eaters and carnivores equally.

HUNAN GLAZED EGGPLANT
with Rice

SERVES 4 AS A SIDE DISH

3 tablespoons rice vinegar

6 tablespoons naturally brewed soy sauce

1 heaping tablespoon sambal

2 tablespoons maple syrup

⅓ cup plus 1 tablespoon canola oil, plus more if needed

5 large or 6 medium Japanese eggplants, cut into 2-inch spears (see Tip)

Kosher salt and freshly ground black pepper

2 bunches scallions, white and green parts, cut into -inch slices, 1 tablespoons of the greens reserved for garnish

2 tablespoons minced garlic

1 tablespoon minced ginger

1 teaspoon toasted sesame oil

1 teaspoon toasted sesame seeds

6 to 8 cups 50-50 White and Brown Rice (page 13)

1 In a small bowl, combine the vinegar, soy sauce, sambal and maple syrup. Stir well and set aside. Line a large plate with paper towels.

2 Heat a wok over high heat. Add the ⅓ cup oil and swirl to coat the pan. When the oil begins to smoke, add the eggplant and season with salt and pepper. Allow one side of the eggplant to brown, then turn and cook on the other side, 3 to 4 minutes total, adding more oil if needed. With a slotted spoon, transfer the eggplant to the paper towels to drain.

3 Heat the wok over high heat. Add the remaining 1 tablespoon oil and swirl to coat. When the oil is hot, add all but the reserved scallions, the garlic and ginger and stir-fry until fragrant, about 1 minute. Add the vinegar mixture and simmer until syrupy, 3 to 4 minutes. Add the eggplant, toss, then add the sesame oil, and a pinch of the sesame seeds and stir-fry until the eggplant is glazed, about 1 minute.

4 Spread the rice on a serving platter and top with the eggplant. Garnish with the reserved scallion greens and remaining sesame seeds and serve.

Ming's tip:

To cut the eggplants into spears, trim and cut each lengthwise into thirds. Cut each length into thirds again and then halve to make 2½-inch spears.

Video tip:

Watch the video to see a demonstration of my simple technique for preparing the eggplants.

To Drink:

An off-dry Gerwürtztraminer, like Trimbach

People think chow mein is an American invention, but it's a venerable Chinese noodle stir-fry. This version celebrates mushrooms—shiitakes, regular button, and oyster—and also includes jicama for crunch. My mom would have made this with fresh water chestnuts, but they're laborious to prep. Jicama provides similar sweetness and crunch and readying it is much easier on the cook. If all you've had is standard chicken chow mein, you must try this.

THREE-MUSHROOM AND JICAMA CHOW MEIN

SERVES 4

12 ounces fresh or 8 ounces dried chow mein or Shanghai noodles

Kosher salt

1 tablespoon plus 1 teaspoon canola oil

2 tablespoons minced garlic

1 tablespoon minced ginger

1 bunch scallions, white and green parts, 2 tablespoons of the greens reserved for garnish

Freshly ground black pepper

⅓ pound shiitake mushrooms, stemmed and cut into ¼-inch slices

⅓ pound button mushrooms, stemmed and thinly sliced

⅓ pound oyster mushrooms, cored, halved if large, and torn into pieces

1 large jicama, peeled and cut into thin strips

1 red bell pepper, diced

1 cup fresh vegetable stock or low-sodium bought

4 tablespoons vegetarian oyster sauce

1 teaspoon toasted sesame oil

To Drink:

A Pinot Noir, like Meiomi, from California

1 Fill a large bowl with water and add ice. Separate the noodles by hand. In a wok, cook the noodles in abundant boiling salted water until al dente, 3 to 4 minutes if fresh, 8 to 10 minutes if dried. Transfer the noodles to the ice water. When cold, drain well, transfer to a plate, and set aside.

2 Heat the wok over high heat. Add the oil and swirl to coat the pan. When the oil is hot, add the garlic, ginger and all but the reserved scallions and stir-fry until fragrant, about 1 minute. Season with salt and black pepper. Add the shiitakes and stir-fry for 2 minutes. Add the 1 teaspoon oil, the button and oyster mushrooms, season with salt and pepper, and stir-fry until all the mushrooms are soft, about 1 minute. Add the jicama and bell pepper, stir-fry for 30 seconds, then add the stock and oyster sauce. Bring to a simmer, add the noodles, toss, and heat through, about 2 minutes.

3 Transfer the chow mein to a serving platter or large pasta bowl. Drizzle with the sesame oil, garnish with the reserved scallion greens, and serve.

Ming's tips:

It's easiest to use a salad spinner for prepping the noodles. Fill its bowl with water and add ice. Drain the cooked noodles in the spinner and return it to the bowl. When the noodles are cold, drain the noodles and spin them dry.

To toss vulnerable ingredients like cooked noodles in a wok or another pan it's best to flip them. Practice flipping using a skillet and rice or beans in your backyard. It doesn't take long to get the knack.

You've probably enjoyed the more traditional version of this dish. It always contains curry and rice noodles, and can also include red-roasted pork, shrimp, and eggs. It is, interestingly, unknown in Singapore, but undoubtedly takes its name from the profusion of Indian restaurants there, which of course serve curries. My version features smoked tofu and crisp bean sprouts, and is every bit as satisfying as meat and seafood curries.

SINGAPORE CURRY TOFU NOODLES

SERVES 4

7 ounces rice vermicelli or bean thread noodles

2½ tablespoons canola oil

1 tablespoon minced garlic

1 tablespoon minced ginger

1 red or green jalapeño pepper, minced

2 tablespoons curry powder, preferably Madras

1 large onion, cut into ¼-inch slices

Kosher salt and freshly ground black pepper

3 large eggs, beaten

1 red bell pepper, cut into ¼-inch strips (see Tip, page 138)

Two 8-ounce packages smoked tofu, or one 14-ounce package firm tofu, cut widthwise into ¼-inch slices

8 ounces bean sprouts, ends trimmed, washed and spun dry

1 tablespoon rice vinegar

1 Put the noodles in a large bowl and fill it with hot water to cover. When the noodles have softened, after about 15 minutes for rice vermicelli, 10 minutes for bean threads, drain and set aside.

2 Add 1 tablespoon oil to the wok, swirl to coat the pan, and heat over high heat. Add the garlic, ginger and jalapeño and stir-fry until aromatic, about 30 seconds. Add the curry powder and onion and stir-fry until softened, about 1 minute. Add another ½ tablespoon oil and season with salt and pepper. Push the onion mixture to one side of the wok and add the remaining 1 tablespoon oil to the other side. When the oil is hot, add the eggs, season with a touch of salt and scramble, stirring, for about 1 minute.

3 Combine the eggs with the onion mixture. Add the bell pepper, tofu and noodles and heat through, tossing, 1 to 2 minutes. Add the bean sprouts and vinegar, season with salt and pepper and heat through, tossing, for 1 to 2 minutes. Transfer to a platter or large bowl and serve.

To Drink:

A Riesling, like Schloss Reinhartshausen, or a lager, like Foster's

This dish has a mixed pedigree. It's based partly on eight treasure rice, a traditional Chinese pudding whose treasures include lotus seeds, dates, and red beans. Its other forbear is *jong zi*, a delicious dim sum made with glutinous rice and pork. I've taken the idea of a savory yet meatless rice dish filled with good things and run with it, creating a great fried rice that's truly a meal-in-one. This is another dish that meat lovers as well as the meat-averse will devour.

EIGHT TREASURE FRIED RICE

SERVES 4

5 tablespoons canola oil
4 large eggs, beaten
Kosher salt
1 tablespoon minced garlic
1 tablespoon minced ginger
1 serrano chile, minced
1 large zucchini, diced
1 bunch scallions, white and green
   parts, thinly sliced, 1 tablespoon of
   the greens reserved for garnish
Freshly ground black pepper
1/3 pound shiitake mushrooms,
   stemmed and cut into 1/8-inch slices
2 tablespoons wheat-free tamari
1 cup shelled edamame
7 cups 50-50 White and Brown Rice,
   cooked and cooled (page 13)
2 tablespoons toasted sesame seeds

1 Line a large plate with paper towels. Heat a wok over high heat. Add 4 tablespoons of the oil and swirl to coat. When the oil is hot, add the eggs and season with salt. When the eggs puff, stir vigorously, then transfer the eggs to the paper towels to drain.

2 Add the remaining 1 tablespoon oil to the wok, swirl to coat, and heat over high heat. When the oil is hot add the garlic, ginger and chile and stir-fry until aromatic, about 30 seconds. Lower the heat to medium-high, add the zucchini and all but the reserved scallions and stir-fry until slightly softened, about 1 minute. Season with salt and pepper. Add the shiitakes and tamari and stir-fry until soft, about 2 minutes. Add the edamame and the eggs. Stir to break up the eggs, then add the rice. Stir until heated through, about 2 minutes. Adjust the seasoning with salt and pepper. Transfer to a large serving platter, garnish with the reserved scallion greens and the sesame seeds and serve.

To Drink:

A Chardonnay, like Cameron
Hughes Lot 220

I love tofu because, like a blank canvas, it invites invention. Here, it's shallow-fried then glazed with a garlic, chile and peanut mixture, so it's not only good for you, but totally delicious. I like to use raw peanuts for this, which are then toasted, but feel free to buy roasted unsalted peanuts, and omit the toasting step.

CRISPY TOFU
with Peanut-Garlic Glaze

SERVES 4

Scant ½ cup raw peanuts
  (see headnote)
2 cloves garlic
1 Thai bird chile or serrano chile,
  stemmed, thinly sliced
Kosher salt
Juice of 1 lime
4 tablespoons ketjap manis, or
  2 tablespoons molasses
1 cup rice flour
2 tablespoons cornstarch
Two 12-ounce packages silken tofu,
  cut lengthwise into ½-inch slices
Canola oil for frying
2 tablespoons thinly sliced chives,
  plus more whole chives for garnish

1 Put the peanuts in a medium sauté pan and toast over medium heat, stirring frequently, for 2 minutes. Lower the heat to low and toast until golden, 1 to 2 minutes.

2 Using a mortar and pestle, or in a mini food processor, grind together or process the garlic, chile, and a pinch of salt until smooth. Add the peanuts and grind or process just until the nuts are chopped. If using a mortar and pestle, you may have to grind them in batches. Add the lime juice and ketjap manis and stir or pulse to blend. Add a pinch of salt and set aside.

3 On a large flat plate, combine the rice flour and cornstarch and mix. Season the tofu with salt and dredge on both sides in the flour mixture.

4 Line a large plate with paper towels. Fill a large straight-sided sauté pan with 1 inch of oil. Heat over medium heat to 350°F on a deep-frying thermometer. Working in two batches, if necessary, add the tofu and fry, turning once, until golden, about 6 minutes total. Transfer to the paper towels and sprinkle with salt.

5 Place a few of the whole chives on individual serving plates. Top with the tofu, spoon the glaze over it, sprinkle with the sliced chives and serve.

Video tip:

Watch the video to watch a tutorial on tofu.

To Drink:

A Champagne or sparkling wine,
like Marquis de la Tour Brut

CHAPTER 7

Sweets

When the dessert's homemade, the meal is special. If you're reluctant to make sweets, don't be. The desserts here are as approachable as they are delicious, and bring something new to your table.

Five-Spice Tarte Tatin, for example, takes the traditional dessert of caramelized apples on a buttery crust eastward. Similarly, Lemongrass Panna Cotta's heavenly texture seems even lighter due to its Thai flavoring. And Cardamom Chocolate Cake, a fudgy bittersweet treat, is enhanced by cardamom's warm, spicy-sweet taste.

As a kid my favorite dessert was a hot fudge sundae. The combination of cold ice cream and hot sauce really did it for me. Chocolate Banana Bread Sundaes up the ante on that great treat by adding sliced coconut-flavored banana bread. The recipe also yields a second loaf, which you can use for more sundaes or enjoy on its own.

I was never a cookie freak until I devised Almond Oatmeal Cookies. Their chewy goodness gives chocolate chip cookies a run for their money. Definitely not homey, Mango Rum Granita makes an elegant dessert, but is ridiculously easy to do. It's another sweet that both new and veteran cooks will love.

I first had tarte tatin when working as a sous-chef at restaurant Natasha, in Paris. I watched, fascinated, as its chef, Jean-Marc Forteneau, prepared it. He caramelized apples in a skillet then topped them with pastry. When he inverted the tart onto a plate and the luscious apples were revealed resting *on* the crust, I couldn't have been happier. Until I tasted the tart, which was amazing. My version is all you want from a tarte tatin *plus* it's flavored with five-spice powder, which takes the usual cinnamon-apple combo to a higher, more interesting place. Served warm with vanilla ice cream, this is as good as it gets. No, better.

FIVE-SPICE TARTE TATIN

SERVES 8

CRUST

3 large egg yolks
2½ cups all-purpose flour
2 tablespoons sugar
16 tablespoons (2 sticks) unsalted
  butter, cold, diced

6 Granny Smith apples, peeled,
  cored and quartered
1½ cups sugar
Juice of 1 lemon
2 teaspoons five-spice powder
4 tablespoons (½ stick) unsalted
  butter

1 Make the crust: In a small bowl, combine the egg yolks with ¼ cup very cold water. In a food processor, combine the flour and sugar. Add the butter and pulse until the mixture resembles coarse meal, about 10 seconds. With the processor running, add the egg yolk mixture in a slow, steady stream and process just until the dough holds together and is no longer crumbly. Transfer the dough to a work surface and divide it in half. Make a ball of each half and flatten into discs. Wrap each disc separately in plastic wrap and refrigerate for 1 hour or up to a week. If not using the second dough within that time, wrap it in plastic then in foil, tuck into a resealable plastic bag, and freeze for up to 3 months for another use.

2 In a large bowl, combine the apples, ½ cup of the sugar, the five-spice powder and lemon juice. Toss and let sit for 30 minutes. Drain the apples, reserving 2 tablespoons of the juice.

3 Preheat the oven to 400°F. Melt the butter in a 10-inch cast-iron pan over medium-low heat. Add the remaining 1 cup sugar and the reserved apple juice and cook, stirring constantly, until a light caramel-brown syrup forms, 15 to 20 minutes.

4 Working from the outside in, shingle the apples in the pan. Slide one apple slice to the side and baste the apples, and while keeping a watchful eye, cook until the caramel is dark amber, about 3 minutes. Cook for about another 10 minutes, until the apples are al dente.

5 Place 1 dough disc on a large sheet of parchment paper and roll it out into a circle, about ¼ inch thick, that will fit the pan with about a ¼-inch overhang. Top the apples with the dough, tucking the edges of the dough between the apples and the side of the pan. Bake for 10 minutes, rotate the pan, and bake until the crust is brown, about 10 minutes more.

To Drink:

A Prosecco, like Lunetta,
or a Calvados

6 Remove the tart from the oven and let rest for 20 minutes. Run a knife around the inside edge of the pan to loosen the tart. Top with a serving dish and being careful of the hot caramel, invert the pan and dish. The tart should drop onto the plate easily; if it doesn't, reinvert the pan and place it on the stove over medium-high heat for 1 to 2 minutes to further melt the caramel and help the tart to release. Cut into slices and serve hot, warm or at room temperature.

Ming's tip:

This recipe makes enough dough for two tarts. Use one half and store the other, as the recipe directs, for another tart or quiche.

This is my version of a cake created by Damien "Big D" D'Silva, a linebacker of a chef, who appeared on *Simply Ming*. His cake featured pearl tapioca, whose wonderful texture I love. The pearls are clearly visible in both of our versions, suspended in a cooked egg mixture. I've kicked things up, though, by flavoring the cake with coconut and lime and serving it with papaya. This makes a unique dessert, one I urge you to try.

TAPIOCA COCONUT CAKE

SERVES 10

1 to 2 tablespoons unsalted butter, for greasing the pan
1 to 2 tablespoons turbinado sugar

PUDDING

1 cup small-pearl tapioca
2 cups whole milk
¾ cup dark brown sugar
2 cans (about 14 ounces each) unsweetened coconut milk
Pinch of kosher salt
Juice and zest of 1 lime
3 large eggs
3 large egg yolks

PAPAYA

1 papaya, peeled, seeded and diced
Juice and zest of 1 lime

1 Cut a piece of parchment paper to fit the bottom of a 9-inch springform pan (see Tip). Grease the bottom and the sides of the pan with the butter. Place the parchment paper in the pan and grease with butter. Add the sugar and tilt the pan to coat the sides evenly.

2 Make the pudding. Put the tapioca in a medium bowl and add cold water to cover it. Let the tapioca soak for 1 hour. Drain the tapioca in a large strainer, rinse well under tepid running water and set aside in the strainer.

3 In a large saucepan, combine the milk, brown sugar, coconut milk and salt and bring to a simmer over medium heat. Add the tapioca, stir, lower the heat to medium-low, and simmer, stirring, until the tapioca is translucent but still slightly raw at the center, 1 to 2 minutes. Pour the pudding into a medium sheet pan, add the lime juice and zest, and stir to combine. Let cool for 5 minutes, stirring occasionally, then transfer to a large bowl.

4 Preheat the oven to 350°F. In a medium bowl, combine the eggs and yolks and whisk until just blended. Pour the eggs over the tapioca, fold to combine, and pour into the prepared pan. Bake until the cake is golden brown in spots and still jiggly in the center, 35 to 40 minutes. Transfer to a rack to cool, then refrigerate in the pan for at least 8 hours or overnight.

5 In a medium bowl, combine the papaya and lime juice and zest. Remove the pan ring, place a serving plate on the cake, and invert. Remove the pan bottom, peel off the paper, cut the cake into wedges and serve with the papaya.

Ming's tips:

To cut parchment paper for lining the baking pan, put the pan bottom on a sheet of the paper. With a pen or pencil draw around the bottom, then cut out the circle about ⅛ inch in from the line.

After baking, the cake will seem unset, but will become firm when refrigerated.

To Drink:

A lychee tea, like Blue Ginger's

Panna cotta, that silky, eggless Italian custard, presents a challenge. You need to have enough gelatin in it so it holds its shape, but not so much that the dessert becomes bouncy. This version achieves just the right ethereal texture—and gives an impression of particular lightness due to the refreshing lemongrass. The panna cotta is topped with sliced strawberries, a final elegant touch.

LEMONGRASS PANNA COTTA

SERVES 8

4 stalks lemongrass, white parts only, pounded and cut into ½-inch pieces (see Tip)

2 cups heavy cream, plus more as needed

3 cups whole milk

7 tablespoons sugar

1 vanilla bean, split lengthwise

2½ teaspoons granulated unflavored gelatin

1 pound strawberries, washed, hulled and sliced ¼ inch thick

Juice and zest of 1 lemon

1 A day in advance, fill a large bowl with water and add ice. In a large saucepan, combine the lemongrass, 2 cups cream, the milk and 6 tablespoons of the sugar. Scrape the seeds from the vanilla bean and add to the mixture. Tie the vanilla pod in a loose knot and add that too. Bring all to a simmer over medium heat. Simmer gently, stirring occasionally, for about 5 minutes. Transfer the pot to the water bath. When the mixture has cooled to room temperature, refrigerate overnight in the pot to steep.

2 Combine the gelatin with ⅓ cup room-temperature water in a small nonreactive bowl. Whisk over a small saucepan of simmering water until the gelatin completely dissolves, about 1 minute.

3 Meanwhile, strain the lemongrass mixture into a 4-cup measuring cup, pressing to extract as much liquid as possible. Add additional cream through the strainer to measure 4 cups and return the mixture to the saucepan. Bring the cream to a simmer over medium heat. Add ½ cup of the cream to the gelatin to temper, stir, return the gelatin mixture to the cream, and gently stir to combine. Pour the mixture slowly through a sieve (to break up any bubbles), dividing it among eight 4-ounce ramekins. Refrigerate to set, 8 hours or overnight.

4 In a medium bowl, combine the strawberries, lemon juice and zest, and the remaining 1 tablespoon sugar. Stir and let sit for 15 minutes.

5 To serve, place the ramekins on dessert plates. Top with the strawberries or serve them on the side.

Ming's tip:

Pound the lemongrass stalks with a meat mallet, the side of a big knife, or a small heavy pan. Remove the fibrous inner core at the end of the lemongrass. Cut the stalks lengthwise to break them up further, then cut crosswise into pieces as the recipe directs.

To Drink:

A Moscato d'Asti, like Michele Chiaro Nivole

Here's a sophisticated dessert that's a cinch to make. A granita that's made in the freezer—
no special equipment is needed—it also features one of my favorite fruits, mango, and a touch
of rum, or vanilla if you're serving this to kids or teetotalers. No mangos? Then by all means
use pineapple, or any juicy fruit. (Bananas, for example, won't do.) Light and refreshing, this makes
a particularly good finish to a rich meal.

MANGO RUM GRANITA

SERVES 4

2 ripe mangos, peeled, pitted
  and roughly chopped
6 tablespoons dark rum,
  preferably Gosling's, or
  1 teaspoon vanilla extract
½ cup club soda or sparkling
  water
Juice and zest of 2 oranges
Juice of 1 lime
2 tablespoons honey, plus more
  if needed
Pinch of kosher salt

1 A day in advance, in a food processor or blender, combine the mangos,
4 tablespoons of the rum, the soda, orange and lime juices and 1 tablespoon
of the honey and process until smooth. Taste, and if not sweet enough, add more
honey. Add the salt.

2 Transfer to an 8-inch square glass or metal container—the mixture should make
a layer that is 1 to 1½ inches thick—and freeze overnight.

3 In a small bowl, combine the remaining 2 tablespoons rum, the orange zest
and the remaining 1 tablespoon honey and stir. Cover and set aside while the
granita freezes. Chill 4 martini glasses in the freezer.

4 Using the back of a fork, scrape the frozen granita into the martini glasses.
Place a spoonful of the zest mixture in the center of each and serve.

Ming's tips:

To select a ripe mango, first sniff the fruit—it should be fragrant. Press it gently;
your finger should make an indentation that "bounces back."

If you do omit the rum, the granita will freeze solid. Let it stand for 10 minutes
at room temperature so you'll be able to scrape it into serving glasses.

Video tip:

Watch the video to learn my simple technique for prepping mango.

To Drink:

The dark rum you use for
the granita

If you haven't tried pots de crème, the classic French custard, you must. Its velvety smoothness takes custard about as far as it can go. This version is flavored with coffee, a drink I'm fully behind. I advise you to get maitake coffee to flavor these—it contains maitake mushroom powder, which sounds strange, but isn't; the powder lends no flavor of its own, but reduces the coffee's acidity so the drink is sweeter. Whatever coffee you use, this is a wonderful dessert.

COFFEE POTS DE CRÈME

SERVES 6

2 cups whole milk
¾ cup sugar
¼ cup ground coffee, preferably Maitake (see Tip)
1 vanilla bean, split lengthwise
1 cup heavy cream
7 large egg yolks

1 Line a fine-mesh sieve with cheesecloth. In a large saucepan, combine the milk, half the sugar and the coffee. Scrape the seeds from the vanilla bean into the mixture and add the pod. Bring the mixture to a simmer over medium-high heat, about 3 minutes. Pour through the sieve into a medium bowl and add the cream.

2 Preheat the oven to 300°F. In a large bowl, combine the egg yolks with the remaining sugar and whisk vigorously to dissolve the sugar. Gradually add 1 cup of the hot cream mixture while whisking vigorously, to temper the yolks. Add the remaining cream in a steady stream and whisk to combine.

3 Arrange six 4-ounce ramekins in a roasting pan. Divide the cream mixture among the ramekins and add enough hot water to the pan to come halfway up the side of the ramekins. Bake until set but an area in the center about the size of a nickel still quivers, about 45 minutes. Leave the ramekins in the water bath on the counter for 15 minutes to cool slightly before removing. Cool for 30 minutes then chill in the refrigerator for at least 8 hours or overnight and serve.

Ming's tips:

The pots de crème have a hint-of-coffee taste. For a more pronounced flavor, allow the sweetened coffee mixture to steep for 20 minutes before straining it.

You can use small (about 4-ounce) coffee cups in place of the ramekins. If you do, allow the cooked pots de crème to sit in their water bath for 20 minutes before removing and chilling them.

If you don't have Maitake Coffee on hand, use your favorite medium roast coffee.

To Drink:
Ming Tsai's Maitake Coffee

Chocolate chip cookies, back off! These chewy-gooey almond cookies are the best cookie ever, period. I ate at least sixteen of them on the day we shot the photos for this book, and I'm not usually a cookie lover. The deep sweetness of the brown sugar and the agave syrup, plus the richness of the almonds from the almond flour, make these irresistible. These are the cookies for which a cold milk accompaniment was invented.

ALMOND OATMEAL COOKIES

MAKES 24

1 cup old-fashioned rolled oats
1 cup almond flour
1 cup all-purpose flour
½ teaspoon kosher salt
½ cup (1 stick) unsalted butter
¾ cup dark brown sugar
2 tablespoons agave syrup
   or honey
1 teaspoon baking soda

1 Place two racks in the bottom and middle positions of the oven. Preheat the oven to 350°F. In a large bowl, combine the rolled oats, flours, and salt and set aside. Fill a tea kettle or small saucepan with about 1 cup water and bring to a boil.

2 In a medium saucepan, melt the butter over medium heat. Add the brown sugar and syrup and stir, then add 2 tablespoons of the boiling water. Bring just to a boil, add the baking soda, and whisk to blend. As soon as the mixture bubbles, remove the pan from the heat and continue to whisk until the bubbles subside. Whisk about 1 minute to incorporate air, then pour over the flour mixture. Using a rubber spatula, fold the liquid ingredients into the dry to make a dough.

3 Roll the dough into balls slightly smaller than golf balls. Place 2 inches apart on two cookie sheets and press down to flatten. Bake until lightly browned all over, 7 to 8 minutes. Don't overbake; the cookies should be chewy in the center. Transfer the cookies to a rack and let cool.

Ming's tip:

You can make awesome ice cream sandwiches with these cookies (as pictured). Let the cookies cool completely. Place a generous scoop—about ½ cup—of the flavor-of-your-choice ice cream, or a nondairy equivalent, on the flat side of one cookie. Sandwich with a second one, pressing down to flatten the ice cream into a disc shape. Roll the sides in toasted sliced almonds for extra crunch. Enjoy immediately or wrap them individually in plastic wrap and store in the freezer for a quick treat.

To Drink:

Cold milk or a nondairy drink
like Rice Dream®

This recipe doubles your pleasure. You make exotically flavored coconut and lime banana bread, which is sliced and used in sundaes that also include, besides your favorite ice cream, luscious chocolate ganache. The recipe yields two loaves—enough to make sundaes for a big party—but you can use one loaf only, and half the ganache, for a smaller event, and store the other loaf, and the remaining ganache, for a later day. It's great to have banana bread on hand; I like to let it get stale, slice it, then brown it in butter, or just nibble it as is. These sundaes end any meal with a major bang.

CHOCOLATE BANANA BREAD SUNDAES

MAKES 2 LOAVES; SERVES 16

3 cups all-purpose flour
2 teaspoons baking soda
½ teaspoon kosher salt
1 cup (2 sticks) unsalted butter, at
    room temperature
1½ cups sugar
5 large eggs
1 cup shredded sweetened
    coconut, toasted (see Tip),
    plus ½ cup for garnish
4 very ripe bananas, mashed
2 teaspoons vanilla extract
Zest of 1 lime

GANACHE
8 ounces bittersweet chocolate chips
1 tablespoon unsalted butter
1½ cups heavy cream
1 tablespoon sugar

Ice cream for serving

1 Preheat the oven to 350°F and set a rack in the center. Spray two 9 by 5-inch loaf pans well with nonstick cooking spray. Sift the flour, baking soda and salt into a medium bowl and set aside.

2 In the bowl of an electric mixer, combine the butter and sugar and beat on low speed for 30 seconds to combine. Increase the speed to high and beat until smooth, 1 to 2 minutes. Reduce the speed to medium and add the eggs one at a time, scraping the bowl between additions. Add the 1 cup coconut, the bananas, vanilla and lime zest and mix just until incorporated. Reduce the speed to low, add the flour mixture gradually and beat to combine.

3 Divide the batter evenly among the prepared pans and bake until a skewer inserted in the middle comes out clean, 45 to 55 minutes. Let rest for 10 minutes then transfer to a cooling rack to cool just until warm.

4 Meanwhile, make the ganache: Put the chocolate chips and butter in a medium heatproof bowl. In a medium saucepan, heat the cream over medium heat until it simmers, and whisk in the sugar. When the sugar has dissolved, pour the mixture over the chocolate and butter and let sit for 2 minutes to melt the chocolate, then stir with a spatula to incorporate the chocolate into the cream.

5 Cut the loaves into ½-inch slices and halve each slice on the bias. Place a small scoop of ice cream in the bottom of each sundae bowl, sprinkle with some coconut, and drizzle with the ganache. Place one half of a banana bread slice against one side of each of the bowls. Add a second scoop of ice cream and place a second banana bread half on the opposite side of the bowl. Drizzle with additional ganache, sprinkle with more coconut and serve immediately.

To Drink:
A dark rum, like Gosling's

Test the banana bread loaves frequently, as they go from gooiness at the center to done very quickly.

You can buy toasted coconut, but to make it yourself, preheat the oven to 350°F. Line a baking sheet with parchment paper. Spread shredded sweetened coconut on the sheet in a thin layer and toast, stirring every few minutes and watching carefully, until golden, about 8 minutes.

Refrigerate unused ganache in a glass container with a cover. Warm the ganache in the container in a hot water bath, about 10 minutes, or in the microwave, stirring it with a rubber spatula every 20 seconds, top to bottom, 2 to 3 minutes.

One of our signature Blue Ginger desserts consists of bittersweet chocolate cake accompanied by cardamom-flavored ice cream. Hmmm, I thought, why not add the wonderful cardamom flavor to the cake itself? Thought to dish, and here it is—a fudgy chocolate cake spiced with cardamom. This makes a sophisticated ending to any meal.

CARDAMOM CHOCOLATE CAKE

SERVES 12

¾ cup (4½ ounces) bittersweet chocolate chips

6 ounces unsweetened chocolate, finely chopped

1 cup (2 sticks) unsalted butter, diced

¾ cup plus ⅓ cup sugar

⅛ teaspoon kosher salt

6 large eggs

1 tablespoon ground cardamom

½ cup confectioners' sugar mixed with 1 teaspoon ground cardamom for garnish

1 Preheat the oven to 325°F and place a rack in the middle position. Spray an 8-inch round cake pan with nonstick cooking spray.

2 Fill a medium saucepan half full of water and place over medium heat. In a medium heatproof bowl, combine the chocolates and butter and set aside.

3 In a small saucepan, combine the ¾ cup sugar with ½ cup water and the salt and heat over medium heat just until the sugar has dissolved and the mixture just reaches a simmer, 2 to 3 minutes. Pour the sugar mixture over the chocolates and butter and place over the saucepan to melt the chocolate. Stir the chocolate with a rubber spatula to melt it completely.

4 Meanwhile, in a large bowl, lightly beat the eggs. In a small bowl, combine the ⅓ cup sugar and the cardamom. Gradually whisk the sugar mixture into the eggs and continue whisking to combine well. Drizzle about ½ cup of the chocolate mixture into the egg mixture, stirring, to temper. Fold in the remaining egg mixture until homogenous. Pour the mixture into the prepared pan, place in a larger baking dish and set on the oven rack. Pour enough hot tap water into the larger pan to come halfway up the sides of the cake pan. Bake until a skewer inserted in the middle comes out clean, 50 to 55 minutes.

5 Transfer the cake in the pan to a rack to cool for about 30 minutes. Place a serving plate over the pan, invert, tap the pan a few times to loosen the cake, and unmold. If the cake doesn't unmold, place the pan over low heat just to warm the pan bottom, then unmold.

6 Using a fine-mesh sieve, sprinkle an even layer of the confectioners' sugar mixture on the top of the cake and serve.

To Drink:

A Banyuls, like Les Clos de Paulilles, or another dessert wine

Video tip:

Watch the video to learn my foolproof technique for making this delicious cake.

CHAPTER 8

Cocktails

I'm really excited to include cocktail recipes in a *Simply Ming* cookbook. It's a first, and there's a reason for it. Over the years Blue Ginger cocktails have earned a following. I'm often asked how we make drinks like Pineapple-Thai Basil Champagne Cocktail, Sake Cucumber Martini, and Passion Fruit Mai Thai. Until now, only *we* had the recipes. Now you do, too.

To ensure best cocktails, I offer these tips:

- Whether used for shaking or in drinks, I always buy ice, and advise you to do the same. Bought cubes are uniform, crystal clear and convenient. Buy the biggest cubes you can find and make sure to keep them "dry" by transferring it to a cooler before you make your drinks.

- Chill martini glasses in the freezer, or add ice water to them, swoosh it around, and pour it out. Martinis really need to be glacier-cold. Thin shards of ice on the drink indicate that they're at the proper temperature.

- Shaking is key. Shake drinks until the outside of the shaker is very cold and beaded with sweat, about 20 seconds. You can make up to two drinks in a shaker at a time but no more.

- Syrups used for drinks are made in quantity and can, and should, be stored for later use—please see the recipes.

I can't think of a better preface to a meal than a kir royale. So, being me, I wanted to create my own version. This is it—a wonderful combination of Champagne, pineapple and basil. Though Champagne is first choice, you can use a good bottle of any sparkling wine and you'll still have a great drink.

PINEAPPLE–THAI BASIL CHAMPAGNE COCKTAIL

SERVES 1

PINEAPPLE-THAI BASIL SYRUP

1 cup turbinado sugar

2 cups fresh pineapple, diced

4 large Thai basil sprigs,
    plus 1 for garnish

FOR EACH DRINK

6 ounces chilled dry Champagne

1 tablespoon Pineapple-Thai Basil
    Syrup

1 Overnight or up to 24 hours in advance, make the syrup: In a medium saucepan, combine the sugar, pineapple and 1 cup water. Bring to a simmer over medium heat and simmer until the sugar is dissolved and the pineapple is soft, about 20 minutes. Remove from the heat and let cool for 2 to 3 minutes.

2 Very gently, crush the basil leaves, but not the stems, in your hands. Add to the syrup, remove the pan from the heat and let cool to room temperature, about 30 minutes. Use the syrup immediately or store in the refrigerator in an airtight container.

3 To make the cocktail, spoon 1 tablespoon of the syrup with a handful of pieces of pineapple into a Champagne flute. Slowly pour the Champagne into the flute, garnish with a fresh basil sprig and serve.

Ming's tip:

The syrup recipe yields about 3 cups, enough for 24 drinks. Keep refrigerated in an airtight container for up to 2 weeks. The leftover syrup can be combined with sparkling water or club soda for a non-alchoholic drink, or use the syrup as a garnish for grilled chicken breasts with a squeeze of lime.

Feel free to use a less expensive sparkling wine in this recipe as well.

Video tip:

Watch the video to see my simple technique for prepping pineapple.

We created this terrific martini for Blue Ginger's opening. I've always been a great sake fan, and it seemed only natural to make a martini featuring it, in this case Ty Ku Sake Black. The cucumber adds tantalizing flavor and texture—as you raise the glass to your lips, you smell it before you taste it, and the fragrance invites you to enjoy the drink.

SAKE CUCUMBER MARTINI

SERVES 1

3 ounces sake

2 ounces vodka

One 4-inch length English
cucumber, peeled and
julienned (see Tip)

1 Fill the tumbler of a Boston shaker with ice. Add the sake and vodka and shake until the ice has broken up, about 20 seconds.

2 Strain into a chilled martini glass. Add 4 or 5 pieces of the julienned cucumber and serve.

Ming's tip:

To julienne the cucumber, if there's a rounded end, square it off. Stand the cucumber on one end and cut it into even slices about ¼ inch thick. Stack the slices and cut into ¼-inch strips.

MING.COM/INYOURKITCHEN/
RECIPE75

The inspiration for this drink was *tom kha gai*, the fiery Thai chicken soup with coconut. The "translation," dish to drink, works beautifully—the vodka-based martini features Coco Lopez, lime and tongue-tingling chile. I love the drink's spiciness; it really opens the palate for the meal to come.

SPICY THAI COCONUT MARTINI

SERVES 1

CILANTRO- AND CHILE-INFUSED VODKA

One 750ml bottle premium vodka
1 large bunch cilantro, washed
2 tablespoons gochugaru (Korean chile flakes)

FOR EACH DRINK

2 tablespoons turbinado sugar
½ to 1 teaspoon togarashi, or to taste
1 lime wedge
1 generous tablespoon cream of coconut
¼ ounce Rose's lime juice
3 ounces cilantro and chile-infused vodka

Ming's tip:

The cilantro and chile-Infused vodka makes about 3 cups, enough for 8 drinks.

1 Make the infused vodka: In a tall glass container with a snap-on lid, combine the vodka, cilantro and gochugaru and let stand for 1 hour. Put a funnel into the empty vodka bottle and using a fine-mesh sieve, strain the mixture back into the vodka bottle through the funnel.

2 On a small plate, combine the sugar and togarashi. Fill a martini glass with ice water to chill. When the glass is cold, discard the water. Rub the lime wedge around the glass rim, then dip the rim into the togarashi mixture to coat it.

3 Fill the tumbler of a Boston shaker with ice. Add the cream of coconut, Rose's and infused vodka and shake until the ice has broken up, about 20 seconds. Strain into the glass, garnish with a cilantro leaf taken from the infused vodka, and serve.

MING.COM/INYOURKITCHEN/
RECIPE76

I call this a superfruit cooler. Superfruits, like melon and blueberry, are great for you, and are included in Ty Ku Liqueur and the flavored vodka, both used here. Most important, though, is taste—and in that department, this cocktail excels, due to the liqueur and blueberry vodka, a great marriage. Try this on a hot summer day—or anytime.

SPARKLING BLUEBERRY COCKTAIL

SERVES 1

GINGER SYRUP

2 cups sugar
2 cups fresh ginger, cut into ⅛-inch
   slices (about 2 large hands)

GIMLET MIX

12 ounces sweet and sour mix
4 ounces freshly squeezed lime juice
2 ounces ginger syrup

FOR EACH DRINK

1½ ounces Ty Ku Liqueur
½ ounce blueberry vodka
1 teaspoon gimlet mix
1 teaspoon pomegranate purée
   or syrup
Club soda
1 very thin lime wheel

Ming's tip:

You will have plenty of leftover ginger syrup. Use it to make your own ginger ale by combining it to taste with club soda, ice and a squeeze of lime juice. It's also great for sweetening tea.

1 Make the ginger syrup: In a medium saucepan, combine the sugar, 2 cups water and ginger and bring to a boil over high heat. Lower the heat and simmer until the mixture is reduced by half, 40 to 45 minutes. Strain out the ginger and set aside.

2 Make the gimlet mix: In a Mason jar or other container with a tight-fitting lid, combine the sweet and sour mix, lime juice and ginger syrup. Stir and refrigerate.

3 Fill the tumbler of a Boston shaker with ice. Add the Ty Ku liqueur, vodka, gimlet mix and pomegranate purée. Shake until the shaker is beaded with sweat and very cold to the touch. Taste and adjust any of the ingredients as needed. Pour the liqueur mixture into a highball glass and top with a splash of the club soda, garnish with the lime wheel, and serve.

MING.COM/INYOURKITCHEN/
RECIPE77

As you can tell, I'm a huge Thai basil fan. I also love mojitos, the Cuban cocktail made with rum, lime juice, and sparkling water. A mojito made with a Thai basil base is an instant East-West classic and a guaranteed crowd pleaser.

THAI BASIL MOJITO

SERVES 1

THAI BASIL SYRUP

2 cups turbinado sugar
2 bunches Thai basil

FOR EACH DRINK

4 lime wedges
4 Thai basil leaves
Pinch of turbinado sugar, plus more
  for rimming the glass
2 tablespoons Thai basil syrup
1½ ounces white rum
Club soda
Thai basil sprig

1 A day in advance, make the Thai basil syrup: In a medium saucepan combine the sugar and 2 cups water. Bring to a simmer over medium heat and simmer until the sugar is completely dissolved, 2 to 3 minutes. Remove from the heat, let cool for 2 minutes, then add the basil. Let cool, transfer to a Mason jar and refrigerate overnight. Strain through a fine-mesh sieve and use immediately or store refrigerated in a Mason jar or other container with a tight-fitting lid.

2 Put the 2 lime wedges in the tumbler of a Boston shaker. Add the basil and sugar and muddle to release the lime juice and to crush the basil leaves. Add the syrup, ice, the juice of 1 lime wedge and rum. Shake until the shaker is beaded with sweat and very cold to the touch, about 20 seconds.

3 Pour some sugar onto a small plate. Run the remaining lime wedge around the rim of a rocks glass and dip into the sugar to coat it. Strain the rum mixture into the glass. Top with a splash of the club soda, garnish with the lime wedge used for rimming the glass and the basil sprig, and serve.

Ming's tip:

The Thai basil syrup yields about 2 cups, enough for 15 drinks. You can use leftover syrup to make an non-alcoholic Thai basil iced tea.

Video tip:

Watch the video to learn all about Thai basil.

Elderflower flavoring is fruity and floral. Absolut Wild Tea Vodka, used here, contains just the right amount of it and pairs naturally with cranberries—the "Boston bog" of the drink's name. Ginger beer adds its own complementary touch to this subtly delicious drink.

ELDERFLOWER BOSTON BOG

SERVES 1

CRANBERRY-HONEY SYRUP

One 1-pound bag fresh cranberries
2 cups honey, or as needed

FOR EACH DRINK

2 heaping tablespoons cranberry-
  honey syrup
Juice of 1 lime
2 ounces Absolut Wild Tea Vodka
3 ounces ginger beer, preferably
  Gosling's
1 lime wheel

1 Make the cranberry-honey syrup: Put the cranberries in a medium saucepan. Pour in the honey until it just coats the berries. Bring to a simmer over medium heat, 8 to 10 minutes, remove from the heat, and let cool. Pour into a glass container with a snap-on lid, cover and refrigerate for up to 6 weeks.

2 Fill the tumbler of a Boston shaker with ice. Add the syrup, lime juice, and vodka and shake until the shaker is beaded with sweat and very cold to the touch. Fill a highball glass with ice. Strain the vodka mixture into the glass and top with the ginger beer. Garnish with the lime wheel and serve.

Ming's tip:

You can make a delicious non-alcoholic drink by eliminating the vodka and substituting sparkling water. The cranberry-honey syrup is great on its own over ice cream—you'll have plenty left over, as this recipe yields about 3 cups, enough for 30 to 40 drinks.

MING.COM/INYOURKITCHEN/
RECIPE79

I can't think of a better traditional cocktail than the rum- and Curaçao-based mai tai. So I set about making my own version—one with its own tropical vibe. I instantly thought of including passion fruit, which is too tart in itself, but works beautifully with other ingredients. Pineapple and orange juice plus apricot brandy further expand the fruit palette of this great drink.

PASSION FRUIT MAI TAI

SERVES 1

1 ounce orange juice
1 ounce pineapple juice
2 tablespoons passion fruit purée
¾ ounce gold rum, preferably Gosling's
½ ounce Gosling's Black Seal Rum, plus more for drizzling
½ ounce apricot brandy
½ ounce grenadine

GARNISH

1 pineapple spear (see Tips)
1 maraschino cherry
½ orange slice, notched (see Tips)

1 Fill the tumbler of a Boston shaker with ice. Add the orange and pineapple juices, passion fruit purée, rums, brandy and grenadine. Shake until the shaker is beaded with sweat and very cold to the touch.

2 Fill a highball glass with ice. Strain the rum mixture into the glass and garnish with the pineapple spear, cherry and the orange half-moon. Drizzle dark rum on top and serve.

Ming's tips:

To make pineapple spears, halve a pineapple lengthwise. Cut one half lengthwise into 4 equal pieces then cut each into 4 spears. Trim the spears so they're 1 inch longer than your highball glass. Wrap and refrigerate unused spears, which can be used for desserts or breakfast.

To prepare the orange slices, halve an orange lengthwise, and cut crosswise into ¼-inch half-moons. Notch a half-moon in the center for fitting onto the glass rim.

MING.COM/INYOURKITCHEN/
RECIPE80

Index

Acknowledgments

Both authors would like to thank Kyle Cathie and US publisher and editor Anja Schmidt, whose kind, attentive professionalism has made working with her a joy once again.

Ming Tsai

Thanks to my co-author Arthur Boehm who again, this fourth time, patiently and masterfully, put my passion on paper. A great writer and even better friend.

Many thanks also to chefs Joanne O'Connell and Denise Swidey, who did a spectacular job at a fierce pace for this book. Thanks also to the entire Blue Ginger crew, led by Jonathan Taylor, Tom Woods, Alex Horowitz and Matt Zikesch, and to Michele Fadden and Deanne Steffen. My gratitude as well to Blue Ginger managers Dan Adelson, Deborah Blish and Erika Staaf.

My thanks also for the super assistance provided by Jill Hardy and Lauren Klatsky—for their help with managing logistics, props and other vital matters. And gratitude to Melissa's/World Variety Produce, Inc., T.F. Kinnealey & Co., Captain Marden's Seafoods, Palm Bay International Fine Wine & Spirits, TY KU Premium Sake & Spirits, All-Clad Metalcrafters LLC, T-fal, Core Bamboo, Revol USA and Clarke showrooms for support and for providing their superior products for the shoot.

To the amazing photographer Bill "Billy B" Bettencourt, assisted by prop stylist Aaron Caramanis, Khalilah Ramdene, Lisa Falso and Nina Gallant, many thanks for his perfect photographs. My gratitude also to videographer and media producer Steve D'Onofrio for the videos that help make this book so innovative, and Dan Kuramoto for their music.

Thanks also to my agents at IMG, Sandy Montag and Melissa Baron, for all they've done on my behalf.

Arthur Boehm

Thanks, first, to Ming Tsai, chef and friend, for the great pleasure of working with him again. In our case, more is always more.

Many thanks also to my agent, Joy Tutela of David Black Literary Agency. Gratitude also to Lauren Klatsky for her kind help in preparing the recipes for publication. And thanks again to Tama Starr for her friendship and support.